Ira D. Sankey, James McGranahan, George C. Stebbins

Gospel Hymns No. 5

with standard selections: words only

Ira D. Sankey, James McGranahan, George C. Stebbins

Gospel Hymns No. 5
with standard selections: words only

ISBN/EAN: 9783337888343

Printed in Europe, USA, Canada, Australia, Japan

Cover: Foto ©Lupo / pixelio.de

More available books at **www.hansebooks.com**

GOSPEL HYMNS
No. 5

WITH STANDARD SELECTIONS.

BY

IRA D. SANKEY,

JAMES McGRANAHAN AND GEO. C. STEBBINS.

(WORDS ONLY.)

PUBLISHED BY

The Biglow & Main Co.	The John Church Co.
76 East Ninth St., New York.	74 W. 4th St., Cincinnati, O.
81 Randolph St., Chicago.	13 E. 16th St., New York.

COPYRIGHT, 1887, BY BIGLOW & MAIN AND THE JOHN CHURCH CO.

PREFACE.

This collection, used by Mr. D. L. MOODY, Dr. GEORGE F. PENTECOST, Mr. D. W. WHITTLE. and other Christian workers, contains the latest and best pieces of the compilers, and a large number of the most useful and popular Sacred Songs by many of the leading composers of the day. A few Standard Hymns and Tunes by the best English authors will also be found in this volume, which, together with the fine selection from "Gospel Hymns Consolidated," make a book which we hope will give satisfaction to all who use it. *It contains more new pieces than any of the single numbers that have preceded it.*

     IRA D. SANKEY,
     JAMES McGRANAHAN,
     GEORGE C. STEBBINS.

NOTICE.

Nearly every Hymn and Tune in this Book is Copyrighted. No one will be allowed to print or publish any of them without the written permission of the owners of copyright.

    BIGLOW & MAIN.
    THE JOHN CHURCH CO.

GOSPEL HYMNS.
No. 5.
WITH STANDARD SELECTIONS.

1.

1. MY Saviour's praises I will sing,
And all His love express;
Whose mercies each returning day,
Proclaim His faithfulness.

Cho.—Every day will I bless Thee!
Every day will I bless Thee!
And I will praise, will praise Thy name
Forever and ever!

2 Redeemed by His almighty power,
My Saviour and my King;
My confidence in Him I place,
To Him my soul would cling.

3 On Thee alone, my Saviour, God,
My steadfast hopes depend,
And to Thy holy will my soul
Submissively would bend.

4 Oh, grant Thy Holy Spirit's grace,
And aid my feeble powers,
That gladly I may follow Thee
Thro' all my future hours.

2.

1. "ONWARD, upward, homeward!"
Joyfully I flee
From this world of sorrow,
With my Lord to be;
Onward to the glory,
Upward to the prize,

Homeward to the mansions
  Far above the skies.

REF.—Onward to the glory,
    Upward to the prize,
  Homeward to the mansions,
    Far above the skies.

2 " Onward, upward, homeward!"
  Here I find no rest,
Treading o'er the desert
  Which my Saviour pressed;
" Onward, upward, homeward!"
  I shall soon be there,
Soon its joys and pleasures,
  I, through grace, shall share.

3 " Onward, upward, homeward!"
  Come along with me;
Ye who love the Saviour,
  Bear me company.
" Onward, upward, homeward!"
  Press with vigor on,
Yet a little moment
  And the race is won.

3.

OH, soul toss'd on the billows, afar from friendly land!
Look to Him who holds thee " in The hollow of His hand."

CHO.—In " The hollow of His hand,"
  In the hollow of His hand,
    O, how safe are all who trust Him,
  In " The hollow of His hand."

2 Though the raging winds may drive thee,
  a wreck upon the strand,
Still cling to Him who holds thee in " The hollow of His hand."

3 When strength is spent in toiling, and wearily you stand,
Then rest in Him who holds thee in "The hollow of His hand."

4 When by the swelling Jordan, your feet in sinking sand,
Remember still He holds thee in "The hollow of His hand."

5 And when at last we're gathered, with all the ransomed band,
We'll praise our God who holds us in "The hollow of His hand."

4.

PRAISE Him! praise Him! Jesus, our blessed Redeemer!
Sing, O earth—His wonderful love proclaim!
Hail Him! hail Him! highest archangels in glory;
Strength and honor give to His holy name!
Like a shepherd, Jesus will guard His children,
In His arms He carries them all day long;
Praise Him! praise Him! tell of His excellent greatness,
Praise Him! praise Him! ever in joyful song!

2 Praise Him! praise Him! Jesus, our blessed Redeemer!
For our sins He suffered, and bled, and died;
He, our rock, our hope of eternal salvation,
Hail Him! hail Him! Jesus the crucified.

Sound His praises! Jesus, who bore our sorrows,
  Love unbounded, wonderful, deep, and strong;
Praise Him! etc.

3 Praise Him! praise Him! Jesus, our blessed Redeemer!
  Heav'nly portals, loud with hosanna ring!
Jesus, Saviour, reigneth for ever and ever;
  Crown Him! crown Him! Prophet, and Priest, and King!
Christ is coming! over the world victorious,
  Power and glory unto the Lord belong;
Praise Him! etc.

5.

I KNOW not why God's wondrous grace,
  To me He hath made known,
Nor why—unworthy—of such love
  Redeemed me for His own.

Cho.—But "I know whom I have believed,
  And am persuaded that He is able
To keep that which I've committed
  unto Him against that day."

2 I know not how this saving faith
  To me He did impart,
Nor how believing in His word
  Wrought peace within my heart.

3 I know not how the Spirit moves,
  Convincing men of sin,
Revealing Jesus through the Word,
  Creating faith in Him.

4 I know not what of good or ill
  May be reserved for me,
Of weary ways or golden days,
  Before His face I see.

5 I know not when my Lord may come,
   At night or noonday fair,
Nor when I'll walk the vale with Him,
   Or "meet Him in the air."

6.

BEHOLD a Fountain deep and wide,
   Behold its onward flow;
'Twas opened in the Saviour's side,
   And cleanseth " white as snow,
   And cleanseth white as snow."

Cho.—Come to this Fountain,
      'Tis flowing to-day;
   And all who will may freely come,
      And wash their sins away.

2 From Calvary's cross, where Jesus died
      In sorrow, pain, and woe,
   Burst forth the wondrous crimson tide
      ‖: That cleanseth " white as snow." :‖

3 Oh! may we all the healing power
      Of that bless'd Fountain know;
   Trust only in the precious blood
      ‖: That cleanseth " white as snow.":‖

4 And when at last the message comes,
      And we are called to go,
   Our trust shall still be in the blood
      ‖: That cleanseth " white as snow.":‖

7.

COME with thy sins to the fountain,
   Come with thy burden of grief;
Bury them deep in its waters,
   There thou wilt find a relief.

Cho.—Haste thee away, why wilt thou stay?
      Risk not thy soul on a moment's delay;

Jesus is waiting to save thee,
  Mercy is pleading to-day.

2 Come as thou art to the fountain,
    Jesus is waiting for thee;
  What though thy sins are like crimson,
    White as the snow they shall be.

3 These are the words of the Saviour:
    They who repent and believe,
  They who are willing to trust Him,
    Life at His hands shall receive.

4 Come and be healed at the fountain,
    List to the peace-speaking voice;
  Over a sinner returning
    Now let the angels rejoice.

8.

O CHILD of God, wait patiently
    When dark thy path may be,
And let thy faith lean trustingly
    On Him who cares for thee;
And though the clouds hang drearily
    Upon the brow of night,
Yet in the morning joy will come
    And fill thy soul with light.

2 O child of God, He loveth thee,
    And thou art all His own;
  With gentle hand He leadeth thee,
    Thou dost not walk alone;
  And though thou watchest wearily
    The long and stormy night,
  Yet in the morning joy will come
    And fill thy soul with light.

3 O child of God, how peacefully
    He calms thy fears to rest,
  And draws thee upward tenderly
    Where dwell the pure and blest;

And He who bendeth silently
  Above the gloom of night,
Will take thee home where endless joy
  Shall fill thy soul with light.

9.

REJOICE in the Lord, O let His mercy, cheer,
  He sunders the bands that enthrall;
Redeemed by His blood, why should we ever fear,
  Since Jesus is our "all in all."

Cho.—If God be for us, if God be for us,
    If God be for us, who can be against us;
  Who, who, who, who can be against us, against us?

2 Be strong in the Lord, rejoicing in His might,
  Be loyal and true, day by day;
When evils assail be valiant for the right,
  And He will be our strength, our stay.

3 Confide in His word, His promises so sure,
  In Christ they are "yea, and amen;"
Though earth pass away, they ever shall endure,
  'Tis written o'er and o'er again.

4 Abide in the Lord, secure in His control,
  'Tis life everlasting begun;
To pluck from His hand the weakest, trembling soul,
  It never, never can be done.

10.

O WONDERFUL words of the gospel,
  Oh! wonderful message they bring,
Proclaiming a blessed redemption
  Through Jesus, our Saviour and King.

Cho.—Believe, oh, believe in His mercy,
    That flows like a fountain so free;
      Believe, and receive the redemption
    He offers to you and to me.

2 He came from the throne of His glory,
    And left the bright mansions above,
  The world to redeem from its bondage,
    So great His compassion and love.

3 O come to this wonderful Saviour,
    Come, weary and sorrow-oppressed,
  Behold on the cross how He suffered,
    That you in His kingdom might rest.

4 There's no other refuge but Jesus,
    No shelter where lost ones may fly;
  And now, while He's tenderly calling,
    O "turn ye," "for why will ye die?"

11.

CLOSER, Lord, to Thee I cling,
    Closer still to Thee;
Safe beneath Thy sheltering wing
    I would ever be;
Rude the blast of doubt and sin,
Fierce assaults without, within,
Help me, Lord, the battle win;—
    Closer, Lord, to Thee.

2 Closer yet, O Lord! my Rock,
    Refuge of my soul;
Dread I not the tempest shock,
    Though the billows roll.
Wildest storm cannot alarm,
For to me can come no harm,
Leaning on Thy loving arm;—
    Closer, Lord, to Thee.

3 Closer still, my Help, my Stay,
    Closer, closer still;

Meekly there I learn to say,
"Father, not my will;"
Learn that in affliction's hour,
When the clouds of sorrow lower,
Love directs Thy hand of power;—
Closer, Lord, to Thee.

4 Closer, Lord, to Thee I come,
Light of life Divine;
Through the ever-blessed Son,
Joy and peace are mine;
Let me in Thy love abide,
Keep me ever near Thy side,
In the "Rock of Ages" hide;—
Closer, Lord, to Thee.

12.

"GOD is love!"—His word proclaims it,
Day by day the truth we prove;
Heaven and earth with joy are telling,
Ever telling, "God is Love!"

Cho.—Hallelujah! tell the story,
Sung by angel choirs above;
Sounding forth the mighty chorus—
"God is Light, and God is Love."

2 "God is love!"—Oh! tell it gladly,
How the Saviour from above
Came to seek and save the lost ones,
Showing thus the Father's love.

3 "God is love!"—Oh, boundless mercy—
May we all its fullness prove!
Telling those who sit in darkness,
"God is Light, and God is Love!"

13.

JESUS, my Saviour, to Bethlehem came,
Born in a manger to sorrow and shame;
Oh, it was wonderful—blest be His name!
Seeking for me, for me!

Ref.—Seeking for me, for me!
Seeking for me, for me!
Oh! it was wonderful—blest be His name!
Seeking for me, for me!

2 Jesus, my Saviour, on Calvary's tree,
Paid the great debt, and my soul He set free;
Oh! it was wonderful—how could it be?
Dying for me, for me!

Ref.—Dying for me, for me!
Dying for me, for me!
Oh! it was wonderful—how could it be?
Dying for me, for me!

3 Jesus, my Saviour, the same as of old,
While I was wand'ring afar from the fold,
Gently and long did He plead with my soul,
Calling for me, for me!

Ref.—Calling for me, for me!
Calling for me, for me!
Gently and long did He plead with my soul,
Calling for me, for me!

4 Jesus, my Saviour, shall come from on high.
Sweet is the promise as weary years fly;
Oh! I shall see Him descending the sky,
Coming for me, for me!

Ref.—Coming for me, for me!
Coming for me, for me!
Oh! I shall see Him descending the sky,
Coming for me, for me!

14.

O UT of my bondage, sorrow, and night,
 Jesus, I come, Jesus, I come;
Into Thy freedom, gladness, and light,
 Jesus, I come to Thee;
Out of my sickness into Thy health,
Out of my want and into Thy wealth,
Out of my sin and into Thyself,
 Jesus, I come to Thee.

2 Out of my shameful failure and loss,
 Jesus, I come, Jesus, I come;
Into the glorious gain of Thy cross,
 Jesus, I come to Thee;
Out of earth's sorrows into Thy balm,
Out of life's storms and into Thy calm,
Out of distress to jubilant psalm,
 Jesus, I come to Thee.

3 Out of unrest and arrogant pride,
 Jesus, I come, Jesus, I come;
Into Thy blessed will to abide,
 Jesus, I come to Thee;
Out of myself to dwell in Thy love,
Out of despair into raptures above,
Upward for aye on wings like a dove,
 Jesus, I come to Thee.

4 Out of the fear and dread of the tomb,
 Jesus, I come, Jesus, I come;
Into the joy and light of Thy home,
 Jesus, I come to Thee;
Out of the depths of ruin untold,
Into the peace of Thy sheltering fold,
Ever Thy glorious face to behold,
 Jesus, I come to Thee.

15.

G LORY ever be to Jesus,
 God's own well-beloved Son;

By His grace He hath redeemed us,
" It is finished," all is done.

Cho.—Saved by grace through faith in Jesus,
Saved by His own precious blood,
May we in His love abiding,
Follow on to know the Lord.

2 Oh! the weary days of wand'ring,
Longing, hoping for the light:
These at last lie all behind us,
Jesus is our strength and might.

3 In His safe and holy keeping,
'Neath the shadow of His wing,
Gladly in His love confiding,
May our souls His praises sing.

16.

WHO came down from heaven to earth?
Jesus Christ our Saviour;
Came a child of lowly birth?
Jesus Christ our Saviour.

Cho.—Sound the chorus loud and clear,
He hath brought salvation near,
None so precious, none so dear:
Jesus Christ, our Saviour.

2 Who was lifted on the tree?
Jesus Christ our Saviour;
There to ransom you and me?
Jesus Christ our Saviour.

3 Who hath promised to forgive?
Jesus Christ our Saviour;
Who hath said " Believe and live"?
Jesus Christ our Saviour.

4 Who is now enthroned above?
Jesus Christ our Saviour;
Whom should we obey and love?
Jesus Christ our Saviour.

5 Who again from heaven shall come?
    Jesus Christ our Saviour;
Take to glory all His own?
    Jesus Christ our Saviour.

17.

WE have heard the joyful sound,
    Jesus saves! Jesus saves!
Spread the tidings all around:
    Jesus saves! Jesus saves!
Bear the news to every land,
    Climb the steeps and cross the waves,
Onward! 'tis our Lord's command:
    Jesus saves! Jesus saves!

2 Waft it on the rolling tide:
    Jesus saves! Jesus saves!
Tell to sinners far and wide:
    Jesus saves! Jesus saves!
Sing, ye islands of the sea;
    Echo back, ye ocean caves;
Earth shall keep her jubilee:
    Jesus saves! Jesus saves!

3 Sing above the battle strife:
    Jesus saves! Jesus saves!
By His death and endless life,
    Jesus saves! Jesus saves!
Sing it softly through the gloom,
    When the heart for mercy craves;
Sing in triumph o'er the tomb,
    Jesus saves! Jesus saves!

4 Give the winds a mighty voice:
    Jesus saves! Jesus saves!
Let the nations now rejoice,
    Jesus saves! Jesus saves!
Shout salvation full and free,
    Highest hills and deepest caves;
This our song of victory,
    Jesus saves! Jesus saves!

18.

HE is coming, the "Man of Sorrows,"
  Now exalted on high;
He is coming with loud hosannas,
  In the clouds of the sky.

Cho.—Hallelujah! Hallelujah!
  He is coming again;
    And with joy we shall gather round Him,
  At His coming to reign.

2 He is coming, our loving Saviour,
  Blessed Lamb that was slain;
In the glory of God the Father,
  On the earth He shall reign.

3 He is coming, our Lord and Master,
  Our Redeemer and King;
We shall see Him in all His beauty,
  And His praise we shall sing.

4 He shall gather His chosen people,
  Who are called by His name,
And the ransomed of every nation
  For His own He shall claim.

19.

WHEREVER we may go, by night or day,
A loving voice within doth gently say:
"My son, from every way of sin depart;
Be Satan's slave no more, give Me thy heart!"

Cho.—"Give Me thy heart, give Me thy heart;
  O weary wand'ring child! give Me thy heart."

2 Slight not that voice so kind, but gladly hear,

And choose the Lord to-day, while He is
  near;
He will His pard'ning love to thee impart;
Oh! hear Him calling still, "Give Me thy
  heart!"

3 We may have chosen long from Him to
  roam,
Yet He will welcome us, if we but come;
Oh! may we not delay, but quickly start—
While Jesus sayeth still, "Give Me thy
  heart!"

20.

O LIST to the voice of the Prophet of old,
  Proclaiming in language divine,
The wonderful, wonderful message of truth
  That "they that be wise shall shine."

Cho.—They shall shine as bright as the stars,
    In the firmament jeweled with
      light;
    And they that turn many to righteous-
      ness,
    As the stars forever bright.

2 Though rugged the path where our duty
  may lead,
O why should we ever repine?
When faithful and true is the promise to
  all
That "they that be wise shall shine."

3 The grandeur of wealth, and the temples
  of fame,
Where beauty and splendor combine,
Will perish, forgotten and crumble to dust,
But "they that be wise shall shine."

4 Then let us go forth to the work yet to do
  With zeal that shall never decline,

Be strong in the Lord, and the promise believe
That "they that be wise shall shine."

21.

I BELIEVED in God's wonderful mercy and grace,
Believed in the smile of His reconciled face,
Believed in His message of pardon and peace;
I believed, and I keep on believing.

Cho.—Believe! and the feeling may come or may go,
Believe in the word that was written to show
That all who believe their salvation may know;
Believe, and keep right on believing.

2 I believed in the work of my crucified Lord,
Believed in redemption alone through His blood,
Believed in my Saviour by trusting His word;
I believed, and I keep on believing.

3 I believed in the heart that was opened for me,
Believed in the love flowing blessed and free,
Believed that my sins were all nailed to the tree;
I believed, and I keep on believing.

4 I believed in Himself as the true Living One,
Believed in His presence on high on the throne,
Believed in His coming in glory full soon;
I believed, and I keep on believing.

22.

MEET me there! oh! meet me there,
In the heav'nly world so fair,
Where our Lord has entered in,
And there comes no taint of sin;
With our friends of long ago,
Clad in raiment white as snow,
Such as all the ransom'd wear—
Meet me there! yes, meet me there!

2 Meet me there! oh! meet me there!
Far beyond this world of care;
When this troubled life shall cease,
Meet me where is perfect peace;
Where our sorrows we lay down
For the kingdom and the crown,
Jesus doth a home prepare—
Meet me there! yes, meet me there!

3 Meet me there! oh! meet me there!
No bereavements we shall bear;
There no sighings for the dead,
There no farewell tear is shed;
We shall, safe from all alarms,
Clasp our loved ones in our arms,
And in Jesus' glory share—
Meet me there! yes, meet me there!

23.

O WEARY pilgrim! lift your head:
For joy cometh in the morning!
For God in His own word hath said
That joy cometh in the morning!

CHO.—Joy cometh in the morning!
Joy cometh in the morning!
Weeping may endure for a night,
But joy cometh in the morning!

2 Ye trembling saints, dismiss your fears:
For joy cometh in the morning!

O weeping mourner! dry your tears:
  For joy cometh in the morning!

3 Let every burdened soul look up:
  For joy cometh in the morning!
And every trembling sinner hope:
  For joy cometh in the morning!

4 Our God shall wipe all tears away:
  For joy cometh in the morning!
Sorrow and sighing flee away:
  For joy cometh in the morning!

24.

ARE you ready, are you ready for the coming of the Lord?
Are you living as He bids you in His word?
Are you walking in the light?
Is your hope of heaven bright?
Could you welcome Him to-night?
  Are you ready?

CHO.—Therefore be ye also ready, be ye also ready,
  therefore be ye also ready,
  for in such an hour, such an hour as ye think not,
  the Son of man cometh.

2 Are you waiting, are you waiting for the coming of the King?
Have you bundles of the golden grain to bring?
Can you lay at Jesus' feet
Any gathered sheaves of wheat,
There your blessed Lord to greet?
  Are you ready?

3 Have you risen, have you risen from the heavy midnight sleep?
Have you risen from your slumber long and deep?

Are your garments washed from sin?
Are you cleansed and pure within?
Are you ready for the King?
  Are you ready?

25.

PRAISE the Saviour, ye who know Him;
 Who can tell how much we owe Him?
Gladly let us render to Him
 All we are and have.

2 Jesus is the name that charms us;
He for conflict fits and arms us;
Nothing moves, and nothing harms us;
 When we trust in Him.

3 Trust in Him, ye saints, forever;
He is faithful, changing never;
Neither force nor guile can sever
 Those He loves from Him.

4 Keep us, Lord, oh! keep us cleaving
To Thyself, and still believing,
Till the hour of our receiving
 Promised joys in heaven.

5 Then we shall be where we would be,
Then we shall be what we should be;
Things which are not now, nor could be,
 Then shall be our own.

26.

SHINE on, O Star of beauty,
 Thou Christ enthroned above;
Reflecting in Thy brightness.
Our Father's look of love.

CHO.—Shine on, shine on,
 Thou bright and beautiful Star,
 Shine on, shine on,
 Thou bright and beautiful Star.

2 Shine on, O Star of glory!
   We lift our eyes to Thee;
Beyond the clouds that gather,
   Thy radiant light we see.

3 Shine on, O Star unchanging!
   And guide our pilgrim way,
Until we see the dawning
   Of heav'n's eternal day.

4 And when, with Thy redeemed ones,
   We reach the heavenly shore,
May we with Thee in glory
   Shine on forever more.

27.

FAR, far away in heathen darkness dwelling,
   Millions of souls forever may be lost;
Who, who will go, salvation's story telling,
   Looking to Jesus, heeding not the cost?

Cho.—"All power is given unto me,
   All power is given unto me,
     Go ye into all the world and preach
       the gospel, and lo,
   I am with you alway."

2 See o'er the world the open doors inviting,
   Soldiers of Christ, arise and enter in!
Brethren, awake! our forces all uniting,
   Send forth the gospel, break the chains of sin.

3 "Why will ye die?" the voice of God is calling,
   "Why will ye die?" re-echo in His name;
Jesus hath died to save from death appalling,
   Life and salvation therefore go proclaim.

4 God speed the day when those of every nation
"Glory to God," triumphantly shall sing;
Ransomed, redeemed, rejoicing in salvation,
Shout "Hallelujah for the Lord is King."

28.

I KNOW I love Thee better, Lord,
Than any earthly joy;
For Thou hast given me the peace
Which nothing can destroy.

Cho.—The half has never yet been told,
Of love so full and free!
The half has never yet been told,
The blood—it cleanseth me!

2 I know that Thou art nearer still
Than any earthly throng;
And sweeter is the thought of Thee
Than any lovely song.

3 Thou hast put gladness in my heart;
Then may I well be glad!
Without the secret of Thy love
I could not but be sad.

4 O Saviour, precious Saviour, mine!
What will Thy presence be,
If such a life of joy can crown
Our walk on earth with Thee?

29.

O PRECIOUS word that Jesus said!
The soul that comes to me,
I will in no wise cast him out,
Whoever he may be.

Ref.—Whoever he may be,
Whoever he may be,

I will in no wise cast him out,
  Whoever he may be.

2 O precious word that Jesus said?
  Behold! I am the Door;
And all who enter in by me
  Have life forevermore.

Ref.—Have life forevermore,
  Have life forevermore,
And all who enter in by Me,
  Have life forevermore.

3 O precious word that Jesus said!
  Come, weary souls oppressed,
Come take my yoke and learn of me,
  And I will give you rest.

Ref.—And I will give you rest,
  And I will give you rest,
Come take my yoke and learn of Me,
  And I will give you rest.

4 O precious word that Jesus said!
  The world I overcame;
And they who follow where I lead
  Shall conquer in My Name.

Ref.—Shall conquer in My Name,
  Shall conquer in My Name,
And they who follow where I lead
  Shall conquer in My Name.

30.

WEARY gleaner in the field, poor or plenty be the yield,
  Labor on for the Master, nothing fearing,
There's a promise of reward, at the coming of the Lord,
  Unto all them that love His appearing.

Cho.—Oh! the crown, the glory crown,
    Oh! the happy day is nearing,
  When the crown of rich reward shall
    be given by the Lord
  Unto all them that love His appearing.

2 Jesus now has gone above to complete His
    work of love,
  His return day by day is surely nearing,
  When His own He will receive, and a welcome He will give
  Unto all them that love His appearing.

3 Oh! how light will seem the grief, and the
    toilsome way how brief,
  When a crown in the glory we are wearing,
  Oh! the rapture who can tell, as forever
    there we dwell,
  With redeemed ones that loved His appearing.

31.

WE lift our songs to Thee,
  Our Saviour and our guide,
Oh! make us from our burdens free,
  And keep us near Thy side.

2 We lift our prayers to Thee,
  Who only heareth prayer;
They who on earth do thus agree,
  Shall find Thy blessing there.

3 We lift our faith to Thee,
  Increased by grace divine;
Help us, O Lord, Thy footsteps see,
  And on Thy help recline.

4 We lift our all to Thee,
  For all things, Lord, are Thine;
Take us, and all we have, and see
  Thy likeness in us shine.

32.

I KNOW that my Redeemer lives,
  And has prepared a place for me,
And crowns of victory He gives
  To those who would His children be.

Cho.—Then ask me not to linger long
    Amid the gay and thoughtless throng.
‖: For I am only waiting here
    To hear the summons: "Child, come home.":‖

2 I'm trusting Jesus Christ for all,
  I know His blood now speaks for me;
I'm list'ning for the welcome call,
  To say: "The Master waiteth thee!"

3 I'm now enraptured with the thought,
  I stand and wonder at His love—
That He from heaven to earth was brought,
  To die that I may live above.

4 I know that Jesus soon will come,
  I know the time will not be long,
Till I shall reach my heavenly home,
  And join the everlasting song.

33.

NOT far, not far from the Kingdom,
  Yet in the shadow of sin;
How many are coming and going—
  How few there are entering in!

Ref.—How few there are entering in!
    How few there are entering in!
    How many are coming and going!—
    How few there are entering in!

2 Not far, not far from the Kingdom,
  Where voices whisper and wait;
Too timid to enter in boldly,
  So linger still outside the gate.

3 Away in the dark and the danger,
    Far out in the night and the cold;
There Jesus is waiting to lead you
    So tenderly into His fold.

4 Not far, not far from the Kingdom,
    'Tis only a little space;
But oh, you may still be forever
    Shut out from yon heavenly place.

34.

ONLY a beam of sunshine,
    But oh, it was warm and bright;
The heart of a weary traveler
    Was cheered by its welcome sight.
Only a beam of sunshine
    That fell from the arch above,
And tenderly, softly whispered
    A message of peace and love.

Cho.—Only a word for Jesus,
    Only a whispered prayer
    Over some grief-worn spirit
    May rest like a sunbeam fair.

2 Only a beam of sunshine
    That into a dwelling crept,
Where, over a fading rosebud,
    A mother her vigil kept.
Only a beam of sunshine
    That smiled through her falling tears,
And showed her the bow of promise,
    Forgotten perhaps for years.

3 Only a word for Jesus!
    Oh! speak it in His dear name;
To perishing souls around you
    The message of love proclaim.
Go, like the faithful sunbeam,
    Your mission of joy fulfill;

Remember the Saviour's promise,
That He will be with you still.

35.

AWAKE, my soul! to sound His praise;
Awake, my harp! to sing;
Join, all my powers! the song to raise,
And morning incense bring.

2 Among the people of His care,
And through the nations round,
Glad songs of praise will I prepare,
And there His name resound.

3 Be Thou exalted, O my God!
Above the starry train;
Diffuse Thy heavenly grace abroad,
And teach the world Thy reign.

4 So shall Thy chosen sons rejoice,
And throng Thy courts above;
While sinners hear Thy pardoning voice,
And taste redeeming love.

36.

MY Father is rich in houses and lands,
He holdeth the wealth of the world in His hands!
Of rubies and diamonds, of silver and gold!
His coffers are full—He has riches untold.

Cho.—I'm the child of a King!
The child of a King!
With Jesus, my Saviour,
I'm the child of a King!

2 My Father's own Son, the Saviour of men,
Once wandered o'er earth as the poorest of them;
But now He is reigning forever on high,
And will give me a home in heaven by and by.

3 I once was an outcast stranger on earth,
  A sinner by choice, an alien by birth;
  But I've been adopted, my name's written down,
  An heir to a mansion, a robe, and a crown!

4 A tent or a cottage, why should I care?
  They're building a palace for me over there!
  Though exiled from home, yet still I may sing,
  All glory to God, I'm the child of a King!

37.

SONGS of gladness, never sadness,
  Sing the ransomed ones in heaven:
Anthem swelling, ever telling
  Of the joy of souls forgiven.

REF.—Sweetest music ever swelling
    Through the courts of heaven above;
  Ever singing, ever saying,
    God is Life, and God is Love!

2 Ever sunshine, never shadow,
    Calm, mild, clear, celestial day;
  Ever summer in its brightness,
    Never winter or decay.

3 Ever gazing, loving, praising,
    With the angel hosts above;
  One eternal Hallelujah,
    One eternal song of love.

4 Never sighing, never sinning;
    No distrust, nor doubt, nor fears;
  Through the long, unending ages,
    Through the long, eternal years.

38.

BLESSED assurance, Jesus is mine!
  Oh! what a foretaste of glory divine!

Heir of salvation, purchase of God,
Born of His Spirit, washed in His blood.

Cho.—This is my story, this is my song,
Praising my Saviour all the day long;
This is my story, this is my song,
Praising my Saviour all the day long.

2 Perfect submission, perfect delight,
Visions of rapture now burst on my sight.
Angels descending, bring from above
Echoes of mercy, whispers of love.

3 Perfect submission, all is at rest,
I, in my Saviour, am happy and blest.
Watching and waiting, looking above,
Filled with His goodness, lost in His love.

39.

ALAS! and did my Saviour bleed,
And did my Sovereign die?
Would He devote that sacred head
For such a worm as I?

Cho.—At the cross, at the cross, where I first saw the light,
And the burden of my heart rolled away,
It was there by faith I received my sight,
And now I am happy all the day.

2 Was it for crimes that I have done
He groaned upon the tree?
Amazing pity, grace unknown,
And love beyond degree!

3 But drops of grief can ne'er repay
The debt of love I owe;
Here, Lord, I give myself away,
'Tis all that I can do!

40.

In the shadow of His wings
 There is rest, sweet rest;
There is rest from care and labor,
There is rest for friend and neighbor;
In the shadow of His wings
There is rest, sweet rest;
In the shadow of His wings
There is rest, *sweet rest.*

Cho.—‖: There is rest, there is peace, there is joy
 In the shadow of His wings. :‖

2 In the shadow of His wings
There is peace, sweet peace;
Peace that passeth understanding,
Peace, sweet peace that knows no ending;
In the shadow of His wings
There is peace, sweet peace;
In the shadow of His wings
There is peace, *sweet peace.*

3 In the shadow of His wings
There is joy, glad joy;
There is joy to tell the story,
Joy exceeding, full of glory;
In the shadow of His wings
There is joy, glad joy;
In the shadow of His wings
There is joy, *glad joy.*

41.

Saviour, breathe an evening blessing,
 Ere repose our spirits seal;
Sin and want we come confessing,
 Thou canst save and Thou canst heal.

2 Though destruction walk around us,
 Though the arrows past us fly;

Angel guards from Thee surround us,
  We are safe if Thou art nigh.
3 Though the night be dark and dreary,
  Darkness cannot hide from Thee;
Thou art He who, never weary,
  Watchest where Thy people be.
4 Should swift death this night o'ertake us,
  And our couch become our tomb,
May the morn in heaven awake us,
  Clad in bright and deathless bloom.

42.

JESUS is tenderly calling thee home—
  Calling to-day, calling to-day;
Why from the sunshine of love wilt thou roam
  Farther and farther away?

REF.—Calling to-day, calling to-day,
    Jesus is calling, is tenderly calling
      to-day.

2 Jesus is calling the weary to rest—
  Calling to-day, calling to-day;
Bring Him thy burden, and thou shalt be blest;
  He will not turn thee away.
3 Jesus is waiting, oh! come to Him now—
  Waiting to-day, waiting to-day;
Come with thy sins, at His feet lowly bow;
  Come, and no longer delay.
4 Jesus is pleading, oh! list to His voice—
  Hear Him to-day, hear Him to-day;
They who believe on His name shall rejoice;
  Quickly arise and away.

43.

SOME one will enter the pearly gate
  By and by, by and by,

Taste of the glories that there await:
  Shall you? shall I?
Some one will travel the streets of gold,
Beautiful visions will there behold,
Feast on the pleasures so long foretold:
  Shall you? shall I?

2 Some one will gladly his cross lay down
  By and by, by and by,
Faithful, approved, shall receive a crown:
  Shall you? shall I?
Some one the glorious King will see,
Ever from sorrow of earth be free,
Happy with Him through eternity:
  Shall you? shall I?

3 Some one will knock when the door is shut
  By and by, by and by,
Hear a voice saying, "I know you not:"
  Shall you? shall I?
Some one will call and shall not be heard,
Vainly will strive when the door is barred,
Some one will fail of the saints' reward:
  Shall you? shall I?

4 Some one will sing the triumphant song
  By and by, by and by,
Join in the praise with the blood-bought throng:
  Shall you? shall I?
Some one will greet on the golden shore
Loved ones of earth who have gone before
Safe in the glory forever more:
  Shall you? shall I?

44.

OH, wondrous Name, by prophets heard
  Long years before His birth;
They saw Him coming from afar,
  The Prince of Peace on earth.

Cho.—The Wonderful! The Counsellor!
　　The Great and Mighty Lord!
　　　The everlasting Prince of Peace!
　　　　The King, the Son of God!

2 O glorious Name, the angels praise,
　　And ransomed saints adore,
　The Name above all other names,
　　Our refuge evermore.

3 O precious Name, exalted high,
　　To Him all power is given;
　Through Him we triumph over sin,
　　By Him we enter heaven.

45.

LET us sing of the love of the Lord,
　　As now to the cross we draw nigh;
Let us sing to the praise of the God of all
　　grace,
　For the love that gave Jesus to die.

Ref.—O the love that gave Jesus to die,
　　　The love that gave Jesus to die;
　　　Praise God, it is mine, this love so divine,
　　　The love that gave Jesus to die.

2 O how great was the love that was shown
　　To us—we can never tell why—
　Not to angels, but *men*, let us praise Him
　　again
　For the love that gave Jesus to die.

3 Now this love unto all God commends,
　　Not one would His mercy pass by;
　"Whosoever shall call," there is pardon
　　for all
　In the love that gave Jesus to die.

4 Who is he that can separate those
　　Whom God doth in love justify;

Whatsoever we need He includes in the deed,
  In the love that gave Jesus to die.

46.

O BROTHER, life's journey beginning,
  With courage and firmness arise ;
Look well to the course thou art choosing,
  Be earnest, be watchful, and wise ;
Remember, two paths are before thee,
  And both, thy attention invite ;
But one leadeth on to destruction—
  The other to joy and delight.

Cho.—God help you to follow His banner,
    And serve Him wherever you go ;
    And when you are tempted, my brother,
    God give you the grace to say "No."

2 O brother, yield not to the tempter,
  No matter what others may do ;
Stand firm in the strength of the Master,
  Be loyal, be faithful, and true ;
Each trial will make you the stronger,
  If you, in the name of the Lord,
Fight manfully under your Leader,
  Obeying the voice of His word.

3 O brother, the Saviour is calling ;
  Beware of the danger of sin ;
Resist not the voice of the Spirit,
  That whispers so gently within ;
God calls you to enter His service,—
  To live for Him here, day by day,
And share by and by in the glory
  That never shall vanish away.

47.

O GOD, our help in ages past,
  Our hope for years to come ;

Our shelter from the stormy blast,
  And our eternal home:—

2 Under the shadow of Thy throne
  Still may we dwell secure;
Sufficient is Thine arm alone,
  And our defence is sure.

3 Before the hills in order stood,
  Or earth received her frame,
From everlasting Thou art God,
  To endless years the same.

4 A thousand ages, in Thy sight,
  Are like an evening gone;
Short as the watch that ends the night,
  Before the rising sun.

48.

FEAR not! God is thy shield,
  And He thy great reward;
His might has won the field;
  Thy strength is in the Lord!

Ref.—Fear not! 'tis God's own voice
    That speaks to thee this word;
  Lift up your head: rejoice
    In Jesus Christ, thy Lord!

2 Fear not! for God has heard
  The cry of thy distress;
The water of His word
  Thy fainting soul shall bless.

3 Fear not! be not dismayed!
  He evermore will be
With thee, to give His aid,
  And He will strengthen thee.

4 Fear not! ye little flock;
  Your Shepherd soon will come,
Give water from the rock,
  And bring you to His home!

49.

"THERE shall be showers of blessing,"
  This is the promise of love;
There shall be seasons refreshing,
  Sent from the Saviour above.

Cho.—Showers of blessing,
  Showers of blessing we need;
Mercy-drops round us are falling,
  But for the showers we plead.

2 " There shall be showers of blessing"—
  Precious reviving again;
Over the hills and the valleys,
  Sound of abundance of rain.

3 " There shall be showers of blessing,"
  Send them upon us, O Lord!
Grant to us now a refreshing,
  Come, and now honor Thy Word.

4 " There shall be showers of blessing,"
  Oh, that to-day they might fall,
Now as to God we're confessing,
  Now as on Jesus we call!

50.

WHEN we gather at last over Jordan,
  And the ransomed in glory we see,
As the numberless sands of the sea-shore—
  What a wonderful sight that will be!

Cho.—Numberless as the sands of the sea-shore!
  Numberless as the sands of the shore!
    Oh! what a sight 'twill be,
      When the ransomed host we see,
  As numberless as the sands of the sea-shore!

2 When we see all the saved of the ages,
  Who from sorrow and trials are free,

Meeting there with a heavenly greeting—
  What a wonderful sight that will be!

3 When we stand by the beautiful river,
   'Neath the shade of the life-giving tree,
  Gazing over the fair land of promise—
   What a wonderful sight that will be!

4 When at last we behold our Redeemer,
   And His glory transcendent we see,
  While as King of all kingdoms He reigneth—
   What a wonderful sight that will be!

51.

ABIDE with me! Fast falls the even-tide,
  The darkness deepens—Lord, with me abide!
 When other helpers fail, and comforts flee,
 Help of the helpless, oh! abide with me!

2 Swift to its close ebbs out life's little day;
  Earth's joys grow dim, its glories pass away;
  Change and decay in all around I see;
  O Thou, who changest not, abide with me!

3 I need Thy presence ev'ry passing hour,
  What but Thy grace can foil the tempter's power?
  Who, like Thyself, my guide and stay can be?
  Through cloud and sunshine, oh, abide with me!

4 Hold Thou Thy cross before my closing eyes;
  Shine through the gloom and point me to the skies;

Heaven's morning breaks and earth's vain
   shadows flee!
In life, in death, O Lord! abide with me!

52.

O PRAISE the Lord with heart and voice,
   With God's own word your doubts
     destroy.
Let those that trust in Thee rejoice,
   Yea, let them shout for joy.

Cho.—Rejoice, rejoice in the Lord,
     Rejoice in the Lord alway;
   Rejoice, rejoice in the Lord,
     and again I say, Rejoice!

2 My life is hid with Thine, O Lord!
   And sheltered from the world's alarm;
  Why should I sink beneath my load
   When leaning on Thine arm.

3 For nothing anxious I shall be,
   But trusting Thee in everything,
  With thanks for every gift from Thee,
   My troubles all take wing.

4 The joys that memory turns to pain,
   I leave for joys that never end;
  My loss I count my richest gain,
   For Christ His joy doth send.

53.

1 O LAND of the blessed! thy shadowless
     skies
   Sometimes in my dreaming I see:
I hear the glad songs that the glorified
    sing
   Steal over Eternity's sea;
Though dark are the shadows that gather
    between,
   I know that thy morning is fair,

I catch but a glimpse of thy glory and light,
  And whisper: "Would God I were there!"

2 O land of the blessed! thy hills of delight
  Sometimes to my vision unfold;
Thy mansions celestial, thy palaces bright,
  Thy bulwarks of jasper and gold;
Dear voices are chanting thy chorus of praise,
  Their forms in thy sunlight are fair;
I look from the valley of shadows below,
  And whisper: "Would God I were there!"

3 Dear home of my Father, thou City of peace,
  No shadow of changing can mar;
How glad are the souls that have tasted thy joy!
  How blest thine inhabitants are!
When, weary of toiling, I think of the day—
  Who knows if its dawning be near?—
When He who doth love me shall call me away
  From all that hath burdened me here.

54.

"NEARER the cross!" my heart can say,
    I am coming nearer;
Nearer the cross from day to day,
    I am coming nearer;
Nearer the cross where Jesus died,
Nearer the fountain's crimson tide,
Nearer my Saviour's wounded side,
    I am coming nearer,
    I am coming nearer.

2 Nearer the Christian's mercy seat,
    I am coming nearer;

Feasting my soul on manna sweet,
 I am coming nearer;
Stronger in faith, more clear I see
Jesus, who gave Himself for me;
Nearer to Him I still would be,
  Still I'm coming nearer,
  Still I'm coming nearer.

3 Nearer in prayer my hope aspires,
 I am coming nearer;
Deeper the love my soul desires,
 I am coming nearer;
Nearer the end of toil and care,
Nearer the joy I long to share,
Nearer the crown I soon shall wear,
  I am coming nearer,
  I am coming nearer.

55.

THE Lord's our Rock, in Him we hide,
 A shelter in the time of storm;
Secure, whatever ill betide,
 A shelter in the time of storm.

Cho.—Oh! Jesus is a Rock in a weary land,
 A weary land, a weary land;
 Oh! Jesus is a Rock in a weary land,
 A shelter in the time of storm.

2 A shade by day, defence by night,
 A shelter in the time of storm;
No fears alarm, no foes affright,
 A shelter in the time of storm.

3 The raging storms may round us beat,
 A shelter in the time of storm;
We'll never leave our safe retreat,
 A shelter in the time of storm.

4 O Rock divine! O Refuge dear!
 A shelter in the time of storm;

Be Thou our helper, ever near,
A shelter in the time of storm.

56.

OH! who is this that cometh
From Edom's crimson plain,
With wounded side, with garments dyed?
Oh! tell me now Thy name.
" I that saw thy soul's distress,
A ransom gave;
I that speak in righteousness,
Mighty to save!"

Cho.—Mighty to save!
Mighty to save!
Lord, I'll trust Thy wondrous love,
" Mighty to save!"

2 Oh! why is Thine apparel
So very deeply dyed?—
Like them that tread the wine-press red?
Oh! why this crimson tide?
" I the wine-press trod alone,
'Neath sorrow's wave;
Of the people there was none
Mighty to save!"

3 O bleeding Lamb, my Saviour,
How couldst Thou bear this shame?
With mercy fraught Thine arm has brought
Salvation in Thy name!
" I the victory have won,
Conquered the grave:
Now the year of joy has come,
Mighty to save!"

57.

LOW in the grave He lay—
Jesus, my Saviour!

Waiting the coming day—
 Jesus, my Lord!

Cho.—Up from the grave He arose,
 With a mighty triumph o'er His foes;
 He arose a Victor from the dark domain,
 And He lives forever with His saints to reign;
 He arose! He arose!
 Hallelujah! Christ arose!

2 Vainly they watch His bed—
 Jesus, my Saviour!
 Vainly they seal the dead—
 Jesus, my Lord!

3 Death cannot keep his prey—
 Jesus, my Saviour!
 He tore the bars away—
 Jesus, my Lord!

58.

SOFTLY and tenderly Jesus is calling,
 Calling for you and for me;
See, on the portals He's waiting and watching,
 Watching for you and for me.

Cho.—Come home; come home,
 Ye who are weary, come home;
 Earnestly, tenderly, Jesus is calling,
 Calling, O sinner, come home!

2 Why should we tarry when Jesus is pleading,
 Pleading for you and for me?
Why should we linger and heed not His mercies,
 Mercies for you and for me?

3 Time is now fleeting, the moments are passing,
    Passing from you and from me;
  Shadows are gathering, death-beds are coming,
    Coming for you and for me.

4 Oh! for the wonderful love He has promised,
    Promised for you and for me;
  Though we have sinned He has mercy and pardon,
    Pardon for you and for me.

59.

O WAND'RING souls! why will you roam
  Away from God, away from home?
  The Saviour calls, O hear Him say,
  Whoever will may come to-day.

Cho.—Whoever will, whoever will,
    Whoever will may come to-day;
    Whoever will may come to-day,
    And drink of the water of life.

2 Behold His hands extended now,
  The dews of night are on His brow;
  He knocks, He calls, He waiteth still;
  Oh, come to Him, whoever will.

3 In simple faith His word believe,
  And His abundant grace receive;
  No love like His the heart can fill,
  Oh, come to Him, whoever will.

4 The "Spirit and the Bride say, Come!"
  And find in Him sweet rest, and home;
  Let Him that heareth, echo still,
  The blessed *whosoever will*.

60.

AFFLICTIONS, though they seem severe,
  In mercy oft are sent;
They stopped the prodigal's career,
  And caused him to repent.

Cho.—"I'll not die here for bread, I'll not die here for bread," he cries;
  "Nor starve in foreign lands;
My father's house has large supplies,
  And bounteous are his hands."

2 "What have I gained by sin?" he said,
  "But hunger, shame, and fear?"
My father's house abounds in bread,
  While I am starving here!

3 "I'll go and tell him all I've done,
  Fall down before his face;
Unworthy to be called his son,
  I'll seek a servant's place."

4 His father saw him coming back;
  He saw, he ran, he smiled,
And threw his arms around the neck
  Of his rebellious child!

5 "O father! I have sinned—forgive!"
  "Enough!" the father said;
"Rejoice, my house; my son's alive
  For whom I mourned as dead!"

6 'Tis thus the Lord His love reveals,
  To call poor sinners home;
More than a father's love He feels,
  And welcomes all that come.

61.

HOW sweet, my Saviour, to repose
  On Thine almighty power!

To feel Thy strength upholding me,
　Through every trying hour!

Cho.—Casting all your care upon Him,
　　Casting all your care upon Him,
　　Casting all your care upon Him,
　for He careth, He careth for you.

2 It is Thy will that I should cast
　　My every care on Thee;
　To Thee refer each rising grief,
　　Each new perplexity;

3 That I should trust Thy loving care
　　And look to Thee alone,
　To calm each troubled thought to rest,
　　In prayer before Thy throne.

4 Why should my heart then be distrest
　　By dread of future ill?
　Or why should unbelieving fear
　　My trembling spirit fill?

62.

IN the harvest field there is work to do,
　For the grain is ripe, and the reapers few,
And the Master's voice bids the workers true
　Heed the call that He gives to-day.

Cho.—Labor on! labor on!
　　　Keep the bright reward in view;
　　For the Master has said,
　　　He will strength renew;
　　Labor on till the close of day!

2 Crowd the garner well with its sheaves all bright,
　Let the song be glad, and the heart be light;

Fill the precious hours, ere the shades of night
Take the place of the golden day.

In the gleaner's path may be rich reward,
Though the time seems long and the labor hard,
For the Master's joy with His chosen shared,
Drives the gloom from the darkest day.

Lo! the Harvest Home, in the realms above
Shall be gained by each who has toiled and strove,
When the Master's voice, in its tones of love,
Calls away to eternal day.

3.

"FOR God so loved!" Oh, wondrous theme!
Oh! wondrous key to wondrous scheme!
A Saviour sent to sinful men—
   Glory to God, the Father!

Ho.—Glory to God, the Father!
   Glory to God, the Father!
   Glory, glory,
   Glory to God, the Father!

In love God gave, in love Christ came,
That man might know the Father's name,
And in the Son salvation claim—
   Glory to God, the Father!

As man He tarried here below,
The power and love of God to show;
To help and heal all human woe—
   Glory to God, the Father!

4 Upon the cross His life He gave,
His people from their sins to save;
For them descended to the grave—
Glory to God; the Father!

5 By God exalted from the dead,
He reigns on high, the living head
Of every soul for whom He bled—
Glory to God, the Father!

64.

O TROUBLED heart! there is a home,
Beyond the reach of toil and care;
A home where changes never come;
Who would not fain be resting there?

Cho.—‖: Oh! wait, meekly wait, and murmur
not; :‖
Oh! wait, oh! wait,
Oh! wait, and murmur not.

2 Yet, when bowed down beneath the load
By heaven allowed, thine earthly lot;
Look up! thou'lt reach that blest abode,
Wait, meekly wait, and murmur not.

3 If in thy path some thorns are found,
Oh! think who bore them on His brow;
If grief thy sorrowing heart has found,
It reached a holier than thou.

4 Toil on, nor deem, though sore it be,
One sigh unheard, one prayer forgot;
The day of rest will dawn for thee;
Wait, meekly wait, and murmur not.

65.

SINNERS Jesus will receive:
Sound this word of grace to all
Who the heavenly pathway leave,
All who linger, all who fall.

REF.—Sing it o'er and o'er again :
  Christ receiveth sinful men ;
  Make the message clear and plain :
  Christ receiveth sinful men.

2 Come, and He will give you rest ;
  Trust Him, for His word is plain ;
He will take the sinfulest ;
  Christ receiveth sinful men.

3 Now my heart condemns me not,
  Pure, before the law I stand ;
He who cleansed me from all spot,
  Satisfied its last demand.

4 Christ receiveth sinful men,
  Even me with all my sin ;
Purged from every spot and stain,
  Heaven with Him I enter in.

66.

THERE'S a Stranger at the door ;
  Let Him in !
He has been there oft before ;
  Let Him in !
Let Him in ere He is gone ;
Let Him in, the Holy One,
Jesus Christ, the Father's Son ;
  Let Him in !

2 Open now to Him your heart ;
  Let Him in !
If you wait He will depart ;
  Let Him in !
Let Him in, He is your Friend ;
And your soul He will defend,
He will keep you to the end ;
  Let Him in !

3 Hear you now His loving voice ?
  Let Him in !

Now, oh! now, make Him your choice;
  Let Him in!
He is standing at the door;
Joy to you He will restore,
And His name you will adore;
  Let Him in!

4 Now admit the heavenly guest;
  Let Him in!
He will make for you a feast;
  Let Him in!
He will speak your sins forgiven,
And when earth-ties all are riven,
He will take you home to heaven;
  Let Him in!

67.

I LOOKED to Jesus in my sin,
  My woe and want confessing;
Undone and lost, I came to Him,
  I sought and found a blessing.

Cho.—"I looked to Him,"
  'Tis true, His "Whosoever;
" He looked on me,
  And we were one forever."

2 I looked to Jesus on the cross,
  For me I saw Him dying;
God's word believed that all my sins
  Were there upon Him lying.

3 I looked to Jesus there on high,
  From death upraised to glory;
I trusted in His power to save,
  Believed the old, old story.

4 He looked on me; oh! look of love!
  My heart by it was broken;
And, with that look of love, He gave
  The Holy Spirit's token.

5 Now one with Christ, I find my peace
In Him to be abiding,
And in His love for all my need,
In child-like faith confiding.

68.

ONCE more, my soul, thy Saviour, thro'
the Word,
Is offered full and free;
And now, O Lord! I must, I must decide;
Shall I accept of Thee?

Cho.—I will! I will! I will, God helping
me,
I will be Thine!
Thy precious blood was shed to purchase me—
I will be wholly Thine!

2 By grace I will Thy mercy now receive,
Thy love my heart hath won;
On Thee, O Christ! I will, I will believe,
And trust in Thee alone!

3 Thou knowest, Lord, how very weak I am,
And how I fear to stray;
For strength to serve I look to Thee alone—
The strength Thou must supply!

4 And now, O Lord! give all with us to-day
The grace to join our song;
And from the heart to gladly with us say:
" I will to Christ belong!"

5 To all who came, when Thou wast here below,
And said, "O Lord! wilt Thou?"
To them "I will," was ever Thy reply;
We rest upon it now.

69.

JESUS, my Lord, to Thee I cry;
  Unless Thou help me I must die:
Oh! bring Thy free salvation nigh,
  And take me as I am.

Cho.—And take me as I am,
  And take me as I am.
    My only plea—Christ died for me!
  Oh! take me as I am.

2 Helpless I am, and full of guilt;
But yet for me Thy blood was spilt,
And Thou canst make me what Thou wilt,
  And take me as I am.

3 No preparation can I make,
My best resolves I only break,
Yet save me for Thine own name's sake,
  And take me as I am.

4 Behold me, Saviour, at Thy feet,
Deal with me as Thou seest meet;
Thy work begin, Thy work complete,
  And take me as I am.

70.

SOULS of men, why will ye scatter
  Like a crowd of frightened sheep?
Foolish hearts! why will ye wander
  From a love so true and deep?
Was there ever kinder Shepherd,
  Half so gentle, half so sweet,
As the Saviour who would have us
  Come and gather round His feet?

2 It is God! His love *looks* mighty,
  But *is* mightier than it seems:
'Tis our Father, and His fondness
  Goes far out beyond our dreams.

There's a wideness in God's mercy,
  Like the wideness of the sea;
There's a kindness in His justice,
  Which is more than liberty.

3 There is no place where earth's sorrows
  Are more felt than up in heaven;
There is no place where earth's failings
  Have such kindly judgment given.
There is welcome for the sinner,
  And more graces for the good;
There is mercy with the Saviour;
  There is healing in His blood.

4 But we make His love too narrow,
  By false limits of our own;
And we magnify His strictness
  With a zeal He will not own.
There is plentiful redemption
  In the blood that has been shed;
There is joy for all the members
  In the sorrows of the Head.

5 If our love were but more simple
  We should take Him at His word;
And our lives would all be sunshine
  In the sweetness of our Lord.
For the love of God is broader
  Than the measures of man's mind;
And the heart of the Eternal
  Is most wonderfully kind.

71.

IN the land of strangers,
  Whither thou art gone,
Hear a far voice calling,
  "My son! my son!"

CHO.—"Welcome, wanderer, welcome!
  Welcome back to home!

Thou hast wandered far away:
  Come home! come home!"

2 "From the land of hunger,
    Fainting, famished, lone,
  Come to love and gladness,
    My son! my son!"

3 "Leave the haunts of riot,
    Wasted, woe-begone,
  Sick at heart and weary,
    My son! my son!"

4 "See the door still open.
    Thou art still my own;
  Eyes of love are on thee,
    My son! my son!"

5 "Far off thou hast wandered;
    Wilt thou farther roam?
  Come, and all is pardoned,
    My son! my son!"

6 "See the well-spread table,
    Unforgotten one!
  Here is rest and plenty,
    My son! my son!"

7 "Thou art friendless, homeless,
    Hopeless, and undone;
  Mine is love unchanging,
    My son! my son!"

72.

ON that bright and golden morning, when the Son of man shall come,
  And the radiance of His glory we shall see;
When from every clime and nation He shall call His people home,
  What a gathering of the ransomed that will be!

Cho.—What a gathering, what a gathering,
  What a gathering of the ransomed
    in the summer land of love ;
What a gathering, what a gathering,
  Of the ransomed in that happy home
    above.

2 When the blest who sleep in Jesus, at His
    bidding shall arise
  From the silence of the grave, and from
    the sea,
  And with bodies all celestial they shall
    meet Him in the skies,
  What a gathering and rejoicing there will
    be.

3 When our eyes behold the city, with its
    many mansions bright,
  And its river, calm and restful, flowing
    free ;
  When the friends that death has parted
    shall in bliss again unite,
  What a gathering and a greeting there
    will be.

4 Oh! the King is surely coming, and the
    time is drawing nigh
  When the blessed day of promise we shall
    see ;
  Then the changing "in a moment," "in
    the twinkling of an eye,"
  And forever in His presence we shall be.

73.

O HEAR my cry, be gracious now to me,
    Come, Great Deliverer, come ;
My soul bowed down, is longing, now, for
    Thee,
  Come, Great Deliverer, come.

Ref.—I've wandered far away o'er mountains cold,
   I've wandered far away from home;
  Oh! take me now, and bring me to Thy fold,
   Come, Great Deliverer, come.

2 I have no place, no shelter for the night,
   Come, Great Deliverer, come;
  One look from Thee would give me life and light,
   Come, Great Deliverer, come.

3 My path is lone, and weary are my feet,
   Come, Great Deliverer, come;
  Mine eyes look up Thy loving smile to meet,
   Come, Great Deliverer, come.

4 Thou wilt not spurn contrition's broken sigh,
   Come, Great Deliverer, come
  Regard my prayer and hear my humble cry,
   Come, Great Deliverer, come.

74.

God be with you till we meet again!
  By His counsels guide, uphold you,
  With His sheep securely fold you;
God be with you till we meet again!

Cho.—Till we meet! Till we meet!
   Till we meet at Jesus' feet;
   Till we meet! Till we meet!
   God be with you till we meet again!

2 God be with you till we meet again!
  'Neath His wings securely hide you,
  Daily manna still provide you;
God be with you till we meet again!

3 God be with you till we meet again!
>   When life's perils thick confound you,
>   Put His loving arms around you;
> God be with you till we meet again!

4 God be with you till we meet again!
>   Keep love's banner floating o'er you,
>   Smite death's threatening wave before you;
> God be with you till we meet again!

75.

1 I MUST walk through the valley and the shadow,
>   But I'll journey in a loving Saviour's care;
> He hath said He will never, never leave me,
>   With His staff He will comfort me there.

Cho.—Through the valley, through the valley,
>   Through the valley and the shadow I must go,
>   But the dark waves of Jordan will not harm me.
>   There is peace in the valley, I know.

2 When I walk through the valley and the shadow,
>   All the weary days of toiling will be o'er;
> For the strong arms of Jesus will enfold me,
>   And with Him I shall sorrow no more.

3 Though I walk through the valley and the shadow,
>   Yet the glory of the dawning I shall see;
> I shall join in the anthems over Jordan,
>   Where the loved ones are waiting for me.

4 I shall walk through the valley and the shadow,
   I shall follow where my Lord has gone before;
Through the mists of the valley He will lead me,
   Till I rest on the Ever-green Shore.

76.

GOD'S almighty arms are round me,
   Peace, peace is mine;
Judgment scenes need not confound me,
   Peace, peace is mine.
Jesus came Himself and sought me!
Sold to Death, He found and bought me!
Then my blessed freedom taught me,
   Peace, peace is mine.

2 While I hear life's rugged billows,
   Peace, peace is mine;
Why suspend my harp on willows?
   Peace, peace is mine.
I may sing with Christ beside me,
Though a thousand ills betide me;
Safely He hath sworn to guide me,
   Peace, peace is mine.

3 Every trial draws Him nearer,
   Peace, peace is mine;
All His strokes but make Him dearer,
   Peace, peace is mine.
Bless I then the hand that smiteth
Gently, and to heal delighteth;
'Tis against *my sins* He fighteth,
   Peace, peace is mine.

4 Welcome every rising sunlight,
   Peace, peace is mine;
Nearer home each rolling midnight,
   Peace, peace is mine.

Death and hell cannot appal me;
Safe in Christ whate'er befall me,
Calmly wait I till He call me,
  Peace, peace is mine.

77.

"LOOK unto Me, and be ye saved,"
  Oh! hear the blest command,
Salvation full! salvation free!
  Proclaim through every land.

Cho.—" Look unto Me and be ye saved,
    all ye ends of the earth,
  for I am God, there is none else,
    Look unto Me, and be ye saved."

2 " Look unto Me," upon the cross,
    O weary, burdened soul!
  'Twas there on Me thy sins were laid,
    Believe, and be made whole.

3 " Look unto Me," thy risen Lord,
    In dark temptation's hour,
  The needful grace I'll freely give,
    To keep from Satan's power.

4 " Look unto Me," and not *within*,
    No help is *there* for thee;
  For pardon, peace, and all thy need
    Look only unto Me.

78.

AS I wandered 'round the homestead,
    Many a dear familiar spot
  Brought within my recollection
    Scenes I'd seemingly forgot;
  There, the orchard—meadow, yonder—
    Here, the deep, old-fashioned well,
  With its old, moss-covered bucket,
    Sent a thrill no tongue can tell.

2 Though the house was held by strangers,
   All remained the same within;
Just as when a child I rambled
   Up and down, and out and in;
To the garret dark ascending—
   Once a source of childish dread—
Peering through the misty cobwebs,
   Lo! I saw my trundle-bed.

3 Quick I drew it from the rubbish,
   Covered o'er with dust so long:
When, behold, I heard in fancy
   Strains of one familiar song,
Often sung by my dear mother
   To me in that trundle-bed;
"Hush, my dear, lie still and slumber!
   Holy angels guard thy bed!"

4 While I listen to the music
   Stealing on in gentle strain,
I am carried back to childhood—
   I am now a child again:
'Tis the hour of my retiring,
   At the dusky eventide;
Near my trundle-bed I'm kneeling,
   As of yore, by mother's side.

5 Hands are on my head so loving,
   As they were in childhood's days;
I, with weary tones, am trying
   To repeat the words she says;
'Tis a prayer in language simple
   As a mother's lips can frame:
"Father, Thou who art in heaven,
   Hallowed, ever, be Thy name."

6 Prayer is over; to my pillow
   With a "good-night!" kiss I creep,
Scarcely waking while I whisper,
   "Now I lay me down to sleep,"

Then my mother, o'er me bending,
  Prays in earnest words, but mild:
" Hear my prayer, O heavenly Father!
  Bless, oh! bless, my precious child!"

7 Yet I am but only dreaming:
  Ne'er I'll be a child again;
Many years has that dear mother
  In the quiet churchyard lain;
But the mem'ry of her counsels,
  O'er my path a light has shed,
Daily calling me to heaven,
  Even from my trundle-bed.

79.

OH, wonderful, wonderful Word of the Lord!
  True wisdom its pages unfold;
And though we may read them a thousand times o'er,
  They never, no never, grow old!
Each line hath a treasure, each promise a pearl,
  That all if they will may secure;
And we know that when time and the world pass away,
  God's Word shall forever endure.

2 Oh, wonderful, wonderful Word of the Lord!
  The lamp that our Father above
So kindly has lighted to teach us the way
  That leads to the arms of His love!
Its warnings, its counsels, are faithful and just;
  Its judgments are perfect and pure;
And we know that when time and the world pass away,
  God's Word shall forever endure.

3 Oh, wonderful, wonderful Word of the
    Lord!
  Our only salvation is there:
It carries conviction down deep in the
    heart,
  And shows us ourselves as we are.
It tells of a Saviour, and points to the cross,
  Where pardon we now may secure;
For we know that when time and the world
    pass away,
  God's Word shall forever endure.

4 Oh, wonderful, wonderful Word of the
    Lord!
  The hope of our friends in the past;
Its truth, where so firmly they anchored
    their trust,
  Though ages eternal shall last.
Oh, wonderful, wonderful Word of the
    Lord!
  Unchanging, abiding and sure;
For we know that when time and the world
    pass away,
  God's Word shall forever endure.

80.

There is no name so sweet on earth,
  No name so sweet in heaven,
The name, before His wondrous birth,
  To Christ the Saviour given.

Ref.—We love to sing of Christ, our King,
    And hail Him blessed Jesus!
  For there's no word ear ever heard
    So dear, so sweet, as "Jesus!"

2 And when He hung upon the tree
    They wrote this name above Him
  That all might see the reason we
    For evermore must love Him.

3 So now, upon His Father's throne—
  Almighty to release us
From sin and pain—He ever reigns,
  The Prince and Saviour, Jesus.

4 O Jesus! by that matchless Name
  Thy grace shall fail us never
To-day as yesterday the same,
  Thou art the same for ever!

81.

HO, reapers in the whitened harvest!
  Oft feeble, faint, and few,
Come, wait upon the blessed Master,
  Our strength He will renew.

Cho.—For they that wait upon the Lord shall
    renew their strength,
  They shall mount up with wings,
  they shall mount up with wings
    as eagles:
‖: They shall run and not be weary,
  They shall walk and not faint. :‖

2 Too oft aweary and discouraged,
  We pour a sad complaint;
Believing in a *living* Saviour,
  Why should we ever faint?

3 Rejoice, for He is with us alway,
  Lo, even to the end!
Look up, take courage and go forward,
  All needed grace He'll send.

82.

WOULD we be joyful in the Lord?
  Then count the riches o'er
Revealed to faith within His Word,
  And note the boundless store.

Cho.—There is pardon, peace, and power,
    And purity, and Paradise;

With all of these in Christ for me,
  Let joyful songs of praise to Him arise!

2 For every sin, by grace divine
    A *pardon* free bestowed;
  And with the pardon *peace* is mine,
    The peace in Jesus' blood.

3 Of grace to break the power of sin,
    He gives a full supply;
  The Holy Ghost, the heart within,
    From sin doth *purify*.

4 The *power* to win a soul to God,
    The Spirit, too, imparts;
  And He, the gift of Christ, our Lord,
    Dwells now in all our hearts.

5 These blessings we by faith receive,
    By simple childlike trust;
  In Christ, 'tis God's delight to *give;*
    He promised, and He must.

83.

"NEITHER do I condemn thee,"
    O words of wondrous grace!
  Thy sins were borne upon the cross,
    Believe, and go in peace.

Cho.—"Neither do I condemn thee,"
    O sing it o'er and o'er;
  "Neither do I condemn thee,
    Go and sin no more."

2 "Neither do I condemn thee,"
    For there is therefore now
  No condemnation for thee,
    As at the cross you bow.

3 "Neither do I condemn thee,"
    I came not to condemn;

I came from God to save thee,
　And turn thee from thy sin.
4 " Neither do I condemn thee,"
　O praise the God of grace;
O praise His Son, our Saviour,
　For this His word of peace.

84.

"THOUGH your sins be as scarlet,
　They shall be as white as snow;
Though they be red like crimson,
　They shall be as wool;"
‖:" Though your sins be as scarlet,:‖
‖: They shall be as white as snow.":‖

2 Hear the voice that entreats you,
　Oh! return ye unto God!
He is of great compassion
　And of wondrous love;
‖: Hear the voice that entreats you,:‖
‖: Oh! return ye unto God.:‖

3 He'll forgive your transgressions,
　And remember them no more;
" Look unto Me, ye people,"
　Saith the Lord, your God;
‖: He'll forgive your transgressions,:‖
‖: And remember them no more.:‖

85.

REJOICE, rejoice, believer,
　And let thy joy and glory ever be,
In Him, the Great Deliverer,
　Who gave Himself a sacrifice for thee.
CHO.—Rejoice, believer, rejoice and sing of
　　　Him who lives for ever,
　Thy great High Priest and Kin

2 Rejoice in thy Redeemer,
　Thou hast a place that nothing can remove;

He bids thee dwell in safety,
   And rest beneath the shadow of His love.
3 Rejoice, rejoice, believer,
   A home on high is waiting now for thee;
 And there in all His beauty,
   The King of saints with wonder thou shalt see.
4 Rejoice, rejoice, believer,
   Press on to join the happy, happy throng;
 Where soon thy Lord will call thee
   To realms of joy and everlasting song.

86.

OH, hear the joyful message,
   'Tis sounding far and wide;
Good news of full salvation,
   Thro' Him, the Crucified;
God's Word is Truth Eternal;
   Its promise all may claim,
Who look by faith to Jesus,
   And call upon His name.

Cho.—‖: " Whosoever calleth, :‖
   Whosoever calleth on His name
   shall be saved!
‖: Whosoever calleth, :‖
   Whosoever calleth on the Lord
   shall be saved!"

Ye souls that long in darkness
   The path of sin have trod,
Behold, the light of mercy!
   Behold the Lamb of God;
With all your heart believe Him,
   And now the promise claim,
That none shall ever perish,
   Who call upon His name.

3 Ye weary, heavy laden,
   Oppressed with toil and care,

He waits to bid you welcome,
  And all your burdens bear;
A precious gift He offers,
  A gift that all may claim,
Who look to Him believing,
  And call upon His name.

87.

GLORY be to the Father, and to the Son, and to the Holy Ghost;
As it was in the beginning, is now, and ever shall be, world without end.
                          [Amen.

88.

"COME unto Me,"
  It is the Saviour's voice,
The Lord of life, who bids thy heart rejoice;
O weary heart with heavy cares oppress'd,
"Come unto Me," and I will give you rest.

Ref.—‖: "Come unto Me,":‖ "Come unto Me," and I will give you rest."
‖: I will give you rest.:‖

2 Weary with life's long struggle full of pain,
O doubting soul, thy Saviour calls again;
Thy doubts shall vanish and thy sorrows cease,
"Come unto Me," and I will give you peace.

3 Oh, dying man, with guilt and sin dismayed,
With conscience wakened, of thy God afraid;
Twixt hopes and fears—oh, end the anxious strife,
"Come unto Me," and I will give you life.

4 Rest, peace, and life, the flow'rs of deathless bloom,
The Saviour gives us, not beyond the tomb—

But here, and now, on earth, some glimpse is giv'n
Of joys which wait us thro' the gates of heav'n.

89.

SAFE home, safe home in port!
  Rent cordage, shattered deck,
Torn sails, provisions short,
  And only not a wreck:
But, oh! the joy upon the shore,
To tell our voyage perils o'er.

2 The prize, the prize secure!
  The wrestler nearly fell;
Bare all he could endure,
  And bare not always well:
But he may smile at troubles gone
Who sets the victor-garland on!

3 No more the foe can harm!
  No more of leaguered camp,
And cry of night alarm,
  And need of ready lamp:—
And yet how nearly had he failed—
How nearly had that foe prevailed!

4 The exile is at home!
  Oh, nights and days of tears!
Oh, longings not to roam!
  Oh, sins and doubts and fears!
What matters now grief's darkest day,
When God has wiped all tears away!

90.

ON Calvary's brow my Saviour died,
  'Twas there my Lord was crucified:
'Twas on the cross He bled for me,
And purchased there my pardon free.

CHO.—O Calvary! dark Calvary!
  Where Jesus shed His blood for me;

O Calvary! blest Calvary!
 'Twas there my Saviour died for me.

2 'Mid rending rocks and dark'ning skies,
 My Saviour bows His head and dies;
 The opening vail reveals the way
 To heaven's joys and endless day.

3 O Jesus, Lord, how can it be,
 That Thou shouldst give Thy life for me,
 To bear the cross and agony,
 In that dread hour on Calvary?

91.

HOLD Thou my hand; so weak I am, and helpless,
 I dare not take one step without Thy aid;
 Hold Thou my hand; for then, O loving Saviour,
 No dread of ill shall make my soul afraid.

2 Hold thou my hand; and closer, closer draw me
 To Thy dear self—my hope, my joy, my all;
 Hold Thou my hand, lest haply I should wander,
 And missing Thee, my trembling feet should fall.

3 Hold Thou my hand; the way is dark before me
 Without the sunlight of Thy face divine;
 But when by faith I catch its radiant glory,
 What heights of joy, what rapturous songs are mine!

4 Hold Thou my hand, that when I reach the margin

Of that lone river Thou dids't cross for me,
A heavenly light may flash along its waters,
And every wave like crystal bright shall be.

92.

"BE ye strong in the Lord and the power of His might,"
Firmly standing for the truth of His word;
He shall lead you safely through the thickest of the fight,
You shall conquer in the name of the Lord.

Cho.—Firmly stand for the right,
On to vict'ry at the King's command;
For the honor of the Lord, and the triumph of His word,
In the strength of the Lord firmly stand.

2 "Be ye strong in the Lord and the power of His might,"
Never turning from the face of the foe;
He will surely by you stand, as you battle for the right,
In the power of His might onward go.

3 "Be ye strong in the Lord and the power of His might,"
For His promises shall never, never fail;
By thy right hand He'll hold thee while battling for the right,
Trusting Him thou shalt for evermore prevail.

93.

ON the Resurrection morning,
Soul and body meet again,

No more sorrow, no more weeping,
  No more pain.

2 Here awhile they must be parted,
    And the flesh its sabbath keep,
  Waiting in a holy stillness,
    Wrapped in sleep.

3 For a space the tired body
    Waits in peace the morning's dawn,
  When there breaks the first and brightest
    Easter morn.

4 On that happy Easter morning
    All the graves their dead restore,
  Father, mother, sister, brother,
    Meet once more.

5 Soul and body, re-united,
    Henceforth nothing shall divide,
  Waking up in Christ's own likeness,
    Satisfied.

94.

Sons of God, beloved in Jesus!
  O the wondrous word of grace;
In His Son the Father sees us,
  And as sons He gives us place.

Cho.—Beloved, now are we the sons of God,
    and it doth not yet appear what we
      shall be:
      but ‖: we know that when He shall appear, :‖
    ‖: we shall be like Him ; :‖
    for we shall see Him as He is.

2 Blessed hope now brightly beaming,
    On our God we soon shall gaze;
  And in light celestial gleaming,
    We shall see our Saviour's face.

3 By the power of grace transforming,
  We shall then His image bear;
Christ His promised word performing,
  We shall then His glory share.

95.

THERE is a name I love to hear;
  I love to sing its worth;
It sounds like music in mine ear—
  The sweetest Name on earth.

2 It tells me of a Saviour's love
   Who died to set me free;
 It tells me of His precious blood—
   The sinner's perfect plea.

3 It tells of One whose loving heart
   Can feel my smallest woe—
 Who in each sorrow bears a part
   That none can bear below.

4 It bids my trembling soul rejoice,
   And dries each rising tear;
 It tells me in a " still small voice,"
   To trust, and not to fear.

96.

BLESSED be the Fountain of blood,
  To a world of sinners revealed;
Blessed be the dear Son of God:
  Only by His stripes we are healed.
Though I've wandered far from His fold,
  Bringing to my heart pain and woe,
Wash me in the Blood of the Lamb,
  And I shall be whiter than snow.

Cho.—||: Whiter than the snow, :||
  Wash me in the Blood of the Lamb,
  And I shall be whiter than snow.

2 Thorny was the crown that He wore,
   And the cross His body o'ercame;

Grievous were the sorrows He bore,
  But He suffered not thus in vain.
May I to that Fountain be led,
  Made to cleanse my sins here below;
Wash me in the Blood that He shed,
  And I shall be whiter than snow.

3 Father, I have wandered from Thee,
  Often has my heart gone astray;
Crimson do my sins seem to me—
  Water cannot wash them away.
Jesus, to that Fountain of Thine,
  Leaning on Thy promise I go;
Cleanse me by Thy washing divine,
  And I shall be whiter than snow.

97.

NOW the day is over,
  Night is drawing nigh,
Shadows of the evening
  Steal across the sky.

2 Jesus, give the weary
    Calm and sweet repose;
  With Thy tenderest blessing
    May our eyelids close.

3 Thro' the long night-watches
    May thine angels spread
  Their white wings above us,
    Watching round each bed.

4 When the morning wakens,
    Then may I arise
  Pure, and fresh, and sinless
    In Thy holy eyes.

5 Glory to the Father,
    Glory to the Son,
  And to Thee, blest Spirit,
    Whilst all ages run.   Amen.

98.

IN the secret of His presence how my soul delights to hide!
Oh, how precious are the lessons which I learn at Jesus' side!
Earthly cares can never vex me, neither trials lay me low;
For when Satan comes to tempt me, to the secret place I go, to the secret place I go.

2 When my soul is faint and thirsty, 'neath the shadow of His wing
There is cool and pleasant shelter, and a fresh and crystal spring;
And my Saviour rests beside me, as we hold communion sweet:
If I tried, I could not utter what He says when thus we meet, what He says when thus we meet.

3 Only this I know: I tell Him all my doubts, my griefs and fears;
Oh, how patiently He listens! and my drooping soul He cheers:
Do you think He ne'er reproves me? what a false friend He would be,
If He never, never told me of the sins which He must see, of the sins which He must see.

4 Would you like to know the sweetness of the secret of the Lord?
Go and hide beneath His shadow: this shall then be your reward;
And whene'er you leave the silence of that happy meeting place,
You must mind and bear the image of the Master in your face, of the Master in your face.

99.

"*TILL He come!*"—Oh, let the words
    Linger on the trembling chords,
Let the "little while" between
In their golden light be seen;
Let us think how heaven and home
Lie beyond that, "*Till He come!*"

2 When the weary ones we love
Enter on that rest above,
When their words of love and cheer
Fall no longer on our ear,
Hush! be ev'ry murmur dumb,
It is only "*Till He come!*"

3 Clouds and darkness round us press;
Would we have one sorrow less?
All the sharpness of the cross,
All that tells the world is loss,
Death, and darkness, and the tomb,
Pain us only "*Till He come!*"

4 See, the feast of love is spread,
Drink the wine and eat the bread;
Sweet memorials, till the Lord
Call us round His heavenly board,
Some from earth, from glory some,
Severed only "*Till He come!*"

100.

ONWARD, Christian soldiers,
    Marching as to war,
With the cross of Jesus
    Going on before.
Christ, the royal Master,
    Leads against the foe;
Forward into battle,
    See, His banners go.

Cho.—Onward, Christian soldiers,
 Marching as to war,
 With the cross of Jesus,
 Going on before.

2 Like a mighty army,
 Moves the Church of God:
Brothers, we are treading
 Where the saints have trod.
We are not divided,
 All one body we,
One in hope and doctrine,
 One in charity.

3 Crowns and thrones may perish,
 Kingdoms rise and wane,
But the Church of Jesus
 Constant will remain.
Gates of hell can never
 'Gainst that Church prevail:
We have Christ's own promise,
 And that cannot fail.

4 Onward, then, ye faithful,
 Join our happy throng,
Blend with ours your voices,
 In the triumph-song:
Glory, laud, and honor,
 Unto Christ the King:
This, thro' countless ages,
 Men and angels sing.

101.

JESUS Saviour, pilot me,
 Over life's tempestuous sea;
Unknown waves before me roll,
Hiding rock and treach'rous shoal;
Chart and compass come from Thee:
Jesus, Saviour, pilot me.

2 As a mother stills her child,
Thou canst hush the ocean wild;

Boist'rous waves obey Thy will,
When Thou say'st to them "Be still!"
Wondrous Sov'reign of the sea,
Jesus, Saviour, pilot me.

3 When at last I near the shore,
And the fearful breakers roar
'Twixt me and the peaceful rest,
Then, while leaning on Thy breast,
May I hear Thee say to me,
"Fear not, I will pilot thee!"

102.

I'VE found a friend in Jesus,—He's everything to me;
  He's the fairest of ten thousand to my soul!
The "Lily of the Valley," in Him alone I see,—
  All I need to cleanse and make me fully whole;
In sorrow He's my comfort, in trouble He's my stay;
  He tells me ev'ry care on Him to roll;
He's the "Lily of the Valley," the bright and morning Star;
  He's the fairest of ten thousand to my soul!

Cho.—In sorrow He's my comfort, in trouble He's my stay;
  He tells me ev'ry care on Him to roll;
He's the "Lily of the Valley," the bright and morning Star;
  He's the fairest of ten thousand to my soul!

2 He all my grief has taken, and all my sorrows borne;
  In temptation He's my strong and mighty tower;

I've all for Him forsaken, I've all my idols torn
From my heart, and now He keeps me by His power.
Tho' all the world forsake me, and Satan tempts me sore,
Thro' Jesus I shall safely reach the goal;
He's the "Lily of the Valley," the bright and morning Star;
He's the fairest of ten thousand to my soul!

3 He'll never, never leave me, nor yet forsake me here,
While I live by faith, and do His blessed will;
A wall of fire about me, I've nothing now to fear:
With His manna He my hungry soul shall fill.
When crown'd at last in glory, I'll see His blessed face,
Where rivers of delight shall ever roll;
He's the "Lily of the Valley," the bright and morning Star;
He's the fairest of ten thousand to my soul!

103.

JESUS, the very tho't of Thee,
  With sweetness fills my breast;
But sweeter far Thy face to see,
  And in Thy presence rest.

2 Nor voice can sing, nor heart can frame,
  Nor can the mem'ry find,
A sweeter sound than Thy blest name,
  O Saviour of mankind!

3 Oh, hope of every contrite heart!
  Oh, joy of all the meek!

To those who fall, how kind thou art!
  How good to those who seek.

4 And those who find Thee, find a bliss
  Nor tongue nor pen can show;
The love of Jesus, what it is
  None but His loved ones know.

5 Jesus! our only joy be Thou,
  As Thou are prize wilt be;
Jesus! be Thou our glory now,
  And through eternity.

104.

LIKE wand'ring sheep o'er mountains cold,
  Since all have gone astray;
To "Life" and peace within the fold,
  How may I find the way?

CHO.—‖:"I am the way, the truth, and the life;
  No man cometh unto the Father but by Me." :‖

2 Bewildered oft with doubt and care,
  To God I fain would go;
While many cry "Lo here! Lo there!"
  The truth how may I know?

3 To Christ the WAY, the TRUTH, the LIFE,
  I come, no more to roam;
He'll guide me to my "Father's house,"
  To my Eternal home.

105.

HAVE faith in God; what can there be;
  For Him too hard to do for thee?
He gave His Son; now all is free;
  Have faith, have faith in God.

2 Have faith thy pardon to believe,
  Let God's own word thy fears relieve;
Have faith the Spirit to receive;
  Have faith, have faith in God.

3 Have faith in God, and trust His might
That He will conquer as you fight,
And give the triumph to the right;
　Have faith, have faith in God.

4 Have faith in God; press near His side;
Thy troubled soul trust Him to guide;
In life, in death, whate'er betide,
　Have faith, have faith in God.

106.

WE shall reach the summer land,
　　Some sweet day, by and by;
We shall press the golden strand,
　Some sweet day, by and by;
Oh, the loved ones watching there,
By the tree of life so fair,
Till we come their joy to share,
　Some sweet day, by and by.

REF.—By and by, some sweet day,
　　We shall meet our lov'd ones gone,
　Some sweet day, by and by.

2 At the crystal river's brink,
　Some sweet day, by and by,
We shall find each broken link,
　Some sweet day, by and by;
Then the star that, fading here,
Left our hearts and homes so drear,
We shall see more bright and clear,
　Some sweet day, by and by.

3 Oh, these parting scenes will end,
　Some sweet day, by and by;
We shall gather friend with friend,
　Some sweet day, by and by;
There before our Father's throne,
When the mists and clouds have flown,
We shall know as we are known,
　Some sweet day, by and by.

07.

MY Jesus, as Thou wilt;
  Oh, may Thy will be mine;
Into Thy hand of love
  I would my all resign:
Thro' sorrow or thro' joy,
  Conduct me as Thine own,
And help me still to say,
  My Lord, Thy will be done.

2 My Jesus, as Thou wilt;
  Tho' seen thro' many a tear,
Let not my star of hope
  Grow dim or disappear:
Since Thou on earth hast wept,
  And sorrowed oft alone,
If I must weep with Thee,
  My Lord, Thy will be done.

3 My Jesus, as Thou wilt;
  All shall be well for me;
Each changing future scene
  I gladly trust with Thee:
Straight to my home above
  I travel calmly on,
And sing, in life or death,—
  My Lord, Thy will be done.

08.

OH, what will you do with Jesus?
  The call comes low and sweet;
As tenderly He bids you
  Your burdens lay at His feet;
Oh, soul so sad and weary,
  That sweet voice speaks to Thee;
Then what will you do with Jesus?
  Oh, what shall the answer be?

REF.—‖: What shall the answer be? ‖:
  What will you do with Jesus?
  Oh, what shall the answer be?

2 Oh, what will you do with Jesus?
　　The call comes loud and clear;
　The solemn words are sounding
　　In every listening ear;
　Immortal life's in the question,
　　And joy thro' eternity;
　Then what will you do with Jesus?
　　Oh, what shall the answer be?

3 Oh, think of the King of Glory,
　　From heaven to earth come down,
　His life so pure and holy,
　　His death, His cross, His crown;
　Of His divine compassion,
　　His sacrifice for thee;
　Then what will you do with Jesus?
　　Oh, what shall the answer be?

109.

LAB'RERS of Christ, arise,
　　And gird you for the toil;
　The dew of promise from the skies
　　Already cheers the soil.

2　Go where the sick recline,
　　Where mourning hearts deplore;
　And where the sons of sorrow pine,
　　Dispense your hallowed lore.

3 Be faith, which looks above,
　　With prayer, your constant guest,
　And wrap the Saviour's changeless love
　　A mantle round your breast.

4 So shall you share the wealth
　　That earth may ne'er despoil,
　And the blest gospel's saving health
　　Repay your arduous toil.

110.

GOD calling yet! shall I not hear?
　　Earth's pleasures shall I still hold dear?

Shall life's swift passing years all fly,
And still my soul in slumber lie?

CHO.—‖: Calling, oh, hear Him :‖
God is calling yet, oh, hear Him calling, calling,
‖: Calling, oh, hear Him :‖
God is calling yet, oh, hear Him calling yet.

God calling yet! shall I not rise?
Can I His loving voice despise,
And basely His kind care repay?
He calls me still; can I delay?

God calling yet! and shall He knock,
And I my heart the closer lock?
He still is waiting to receive,
And shall I dare His spirit grieve?

God calling yet! and shall I give
No heed, but still in bondage live?
I wait, but He does not forsake;
He calls me still; my heart, awake!

God calling yet! I cannot stay;
My heart I yield without delay:
Vain world, farewell, from thee I part;
The voice of God has reached my heart.

111.

OH cease, my wandering soul,
 On restless wing to roam;
All this wide world, to either pole,
 Hath not for thee a home.

2 Behold the ark of God!
 Behold the open door!
Oh, haste to gain that dear abode,
 And rove, my soul, no more.

3 There safe thou shalt abide,
 There sweet shall be thy rest;

And every longing satisfied,
　With full salvation blest.

4 Ah, no! I all forsake,
　My all to Thee resign;
Gracious Redeemer, take, oh take
　And seal me ever Thine.

112.

GOD loved a world of sinners,
　For them He gave His Son;
And whosoe'er receives Him,
　He saves them, every one;
He came to bring salvation,
　To bear our sins away,
That we with Him in glory
　Might live thro' endless day.

Cho.—‖: " How shall we escape if we neglect
　　so great salvation? :‖
　neglect so great salvation?"

2 Behold the bleeding Saviour
　Upon the cruel tree,—
The Just condemned, forsaken—
　He dies for you and me;
The "Son of God" beloved,
　For us a curse was made;
That we might have redemption,
　The awful price He paid.

3 God loves the vilest sinner,
　But hates the smallest sin;
Then who shall see His kingdom?
　Or who can enter in?
"The precious blood of Jesus"—
　Let ev'ry creature know—
Can make the "chief of sinners"
　Full whiter than the snow.

4 Return to God, O wand'rer,
　Thy purchased pardon take;

Thy sins He'll not remember,
  For thy Redeemer's sake;
He'll cast them all behind Him,
  Or 'neath the deepest sea,
And love us ever freely
  Thro'out Eternity.

113.

COME to Jesus! come away!
  Forsake thy sins,—oh, why delay
His arms are open night and day;
  He waits to welcome thee!

2 Come to Jesus! all is free;
Hark! how He calls, "Come unto Me
I cast out none, I'll pardon thee,"
  Oh, thou shalt welcome be!

3 Come to Jesus! cling to Him;
He'll keep thee free from paths of sin;
Thou shalt at last a victory win,
  And He will welcome thee!

4 Come to Jesus!—Lord, I come!
Weary of sin, no more I'd roam,
But with my Saviour be at home;
  I know He'll welcome me!

114.

AT the feast of Belshazzar and a thousand of his lords,
While they drank from golden vessels, as the Book of Truth records—
In the night, as they revelled in the royal palace hall,
They were seized with consternation,—
  'twas the Hand upon the wall!

CHO.—‖: 'Tis the hand of God on the wall! :‖
  Shall the record be "Found wanting!"
  Or shall it be "Found trusting!"
  While that hand is writing on the wall?

2 See the brave captive, Daniel, as he stoo[d]
    before the throng,
  And rebuk'd the haughty monarch for hi[s]
    mighty deeds of wrong;
  As he read out the writing—'twas the doo[m]
    of one and all,
  For the kingdom now was finished—sai[d]
    the Hand upon the wall!

3 See the faith, zeal, and courage, that woul[d]
    dare to do the right,
  Which the Spirit gave to Daniel—this th[e]
    secret of his might
  In his home in Judea, or a captive in th[e]
    hall,
  He understood the writing of his God upo[n]
    the wall!

4 So our deeds are recorded—there's a Han[d]
    that's writing now;
  Sinner, give your heart to Jesus—to Hi[s]
    royal mandates bow;
  For the day is approaching—it must com[e]
    to one and all,
  When the sinners' condemnation will b[e]
    written on the wall!

115.

JERUSALEM! my happy home!
  Name ever dear to me!
When shall my labors have an end,
  In joy, and peace, in thee!

2 Oh, when, thou city of my God,
  Shall I thy courts ascend,
Where congregations ne'er break up,
  And Sabbaths have no end?

3 Jerusalem! my happy home!
  My soul still pants for thee;
Then shall my labors have an end,
  When I thy joy shall see.

116.

1 THERE'S a royal banner given for display
To the soldiers of the King;
As an ensign fair we lift it up to-day,
While as ransomed ones we sing.

CHO.—Marching on! Marching on!
For Christ count ev'rything but loss;
And to crown Him King, toil and sing,
'Neath the banner of the cross.

2 Tho' the foe may rage and gather as the flood,
Let the standard be displayed;
And beneath its folds, as soldiers of the Lord,
For the truth be not dismayed!

3 Over land and sea, wherever man may dwell,
Make the glorious tidings known;
Of the crimson banner now the story tell,
While the Lord shall claim His own!

4 When the glory dawns—'tis dawning very near—
It is hast'ning day by day—
Then before our King the foe shall disappear,
And the Cross the world shall sway.

117.

1 I WAS once far away from the Saviour,
And as vile as a sinner could be;
And I wonder'd if Christ the Redeemer
Could save a poor sinner like me.

2 I wandered on in the darkness,
Not a ray of light could I see;
And the tho't filled my heart with sadness,
There's no hope for a sinner like me.

3 And then, in that dark lonely hour,
   A voice sweetly whispered to me,
Saying, Christ the Redeemer has power
   To save a poor sinner like me.

4 I listened: and lo! 'twas the Saviour
   That was speaking so kindly to me;
I cried, "I'm the chief of sinners,
   Thou canst save a poor sinner like me!

5 I then fully trusted in Jesus;
   And oh, what a joy came to me!
My heart was filled with His praises,
   For saving a sinner like me.

6 No longer in darkness I'm walking,
   For the light is now shining on me;
And now unto others I'm telling
   How He saved a poor sinner like me.

7 And when life's journey is over,
   And I the dear Saviour shall see,
I'll praise Him forever and ever,
   For saving a sinner like me.

118.

THERE is a calm beyond life's fitful fever,
   A deep repose, an everlasting rest;
Where white-robed angels welcome the believer,
   Among the blest, among the blest.
There is a home, where all the soul's deep yearnings,
   And silent prayers shall be at last fulfilled;
Where strife and sorrow, murm'rings and heart burnings
   At last are stilled, at last are stilled.

2 There is a Hope, to which the Christian, clinging;
   Is lifted high above life's surging wave;

Finds life in death, and fadeless flowers
 springing
　From the dark grave, from the dark
　 grave.
There is a crown prepared for those who
 love Him;
　The Christian sees it in the distance
　 shine,
Like a bright beacon glittering above him,
　And whispers, "Mine!" and whispers,
　 "Mine!"

3 There is a spotless robe of Christ's own
 weaving;
　Will you not wrap it round your sin-
　 stained soul?
Poor wand'ring child, upon thy past life
 grieving,
　Christ makes thee whole! Christ makes
　 thee whole!

There is a Home, a Harp, a Crown in
 Heaven;—
　Alas! that any should Thy gift refuse!—
The awful choice of life and death is
 given—
　Which wilt thou choose? which wilt thou
　 choose?

119.

There is a stream, whose gentle flow
　Supplies the city of our God;
Life, love, and joy, still gliding thro',
　And wat'ring our divine abode.

2 That sacred stream, Thy holy Word,
　Supports our faith, our fears controls:
Sweet peace Thy promises afford,
　And give new strength to fainting souls.

3 Loud may the troubled ocean roar;
　In sacred peace our souls abide,
While ev'ry nation, ev'ry shore,
　Trembles, and dreads the swelling tide.

120.

A GUILTY soul, by Pharisees of old,
　Was brought accused, alone,
But Jesus said, "Let him without a sin,
　Be first to cast a stone."

Cho.—" There is none righteous, no, not one,
　All, all have sinned,"
　　There is none righteous, for all have
　　　sinned, and come short of the
　　　glory, the glory of God,
||: Come short of the glory,:||
　of the glory of God.

2 A learned Master, Ruler of the Jews,
　God's kingdom could not gain,
With all the lore and culture of the age,
　He "must be born again."

3 "Good Master," pray can aught be lacking
　　yet?
　Thy laws I do obey;
"Go sell and *give*, then come and follow
　　me,"
　But sad he turned away.

121.

JESUS bids us shine with a clear, pure
　　light,
Like a little candle burning in the night;
In the world is darkness; so we must
　　shine,
You in your corner and I in mine.

2 Jesus bids us shine first of all for Him,
　Well He sees and knows it if our light is
　　dim;

He looks down from heaven, He sees us shine,
You in your corner and I in mine.

3 Jesus bids us shine then for all around,
Many kinds of darkness in the world are found;
Sin and want and sorrow; so we must shine,
You in your corner and I in mine.

122.

WHOEVER receiveth the Crucified One,
Whoever believeth on God's only Son,
A free and a perfect salvation shall have:
For He is abundantly able to save.

Cho.—My brother, the Master is calling for thee;
His grace and His mercy are wondrously free;
His blood as a ransom for sinners He gave,
And He is abundantly able to save.

2 Whoever receiveth the message of God,
And trusts in the power of the soul-cleansing blood,
A full and eternal redemption shall have:
For He is both able and willing to save.

3 Whoever repents and forsakes ev'ry sin,
And opens his heart for the Lord to come in,
A present and perfect salvation shall have:
For Jesus is ready this moment to save.

123.

COME, come to Jesus!
He waits to welcome thee,

O wand'rer, eagerly
Come, come to Jesus!

2 Come, come to Jesus!
He waits to ranson thee,
O slave! so willingly,
Come, come to Jesus!

3 Come, come to Jesus!
He waits to lighten thee,
O burdened! trustingly;
Come, come to Jesus!

4 Come, come to Jesus!
He waits to give to thee,
O blind! a vision free;
Come, come to Jesus!

5 Come, come to Jesus!
He waits to shelter thee,
O weary! blessedly
Come, come to Jesus!

6 Come, come to Jesus!
He waits to carry thee,
O lamb! so lovingly,
Come, come to Jesus!

124.

SITTING by the gateway of a palace fair,
Once a child of God was left to die;
By the world neglected, wealth would nothing share;
See the change awaiting there on high,

CHO.—Carried by the angels to the land of rest,
Music sweetly sounding thro' the skies;
Welcomed by the Saviour to the heav'nly feast,
Gathered with the loved in Paradise.

2 What shall be the ending of this life of
    care?
  Oft the question cometh to us all;
  Here upon the pathway hard the burdens
    bear,
  And the burning tears of sorrow fall

3 Follower of Jesus, scanty tho' thy store,
  Treasures, precious treasures wait on
    high;
  Count the trials joyful, soon they'll all
    be o'er;
  Of the change that's coming bye and bye.

4 Upward, then, and onward! onward for
    the Lord;
  Time and talent all in His employ;
  Small may seem the service, sure the great
    reward;
  Here the cross, but there the crown of joy.

125.

O CHRISTIAN trav'ller, fear no more
  The storms which round thee spread;
Nor yet the noontide's sultry beams
  On thy defenceless head.

Cho.—‖: "Fear thou not, for I am with thee:
  Be not dismayed, for I am thy God.":‖

2 Thy Saviour who upon the cross
  Thy full redemption paid,
Will not from thee, His ransomed one,
  Withhold His promised aid.

3 A safe retreat and hiding place
  Thy Saviour will provide;
And sorrow cannot fill thy heart,
  While sheltered at His side.

4 No; in thy darkest days on earth,
  When every joy seems flown,

Believer, thou shalt never tread
The toilsome way alone.

126.

HAVE our hearts grown cold since the days of old?
Have we left our soul's " first love "?
Neither cold nor hot, God commends us not,
Nor our luke-warm ways approve.

Cho.—Repent ye, repent ye, repent ye!
'Tis the call of God to every land;
Repent ye, repent ye, repent ye!
For the kingdom of heaven is at hand.

2 Has the God above our supreme true love?
Have we bowed to Him alway?
Do we own His claim and revere His name,
And observe His holy day?

3 Do we honor those who have soothed our woes?
Have we rendered good for ill?
Are we pure in heart, doing *all* our part
To fulfil the Saviour's will?

4 Are we always true in the thing we do,
In our works, our words, our ways?
Are we quite content with the blessings sent,
Giving God alone the praise?

5 Dare a mortal say—for a single day—
" I have kept Thy law, O God!
Undefiled by sin, I am pure within,
And I need no cleansing blood?"

127.

CLING to the Bible, though all else be taken;
Lose not its promises precious and sure

Souls that are sleeping its echoes awaken,
    Drink from the fountain, so peaceful, so pure.

Cho.—||: Cling to the Bible! :|| Cling to the Bible!
    Our Lamp and Guide.

2 Cling to the Bible, this jewel, this treasure
    Brings to us honor and saves fallen man;
Pearl whose great value no mortal can measure,
    Seek and secure it, O soul, while you can.

3 Lamp for the feet that in by-ways have wander'd,
    Guide for the youth that would otherwise fall;
Hope for the sinner whose best days are squander'd,
    Staff for the aged, and best book of all.

128.

HARK, hark! my soul! angelic songs are swelling
    O'er earth's green fields and ocean's wave-beat shore;
How sweet the truth those blessed strains are telling
    Of that new life when sin shall be no more.

Cho.—Angels, sing on! your faithful watches keeping;
        Sing us sweet fragments of the songs above,
    Till morning's joy shall end the night of weeping,
        And life's long shadows break in cloudless love.

2 Far, far away, like bells at evening pealing,
   The voice of Jesus sounds o'er land and sea;
  And laden souls by thousands meekly stealing,
   Kind Shepherd, turn their weary steps to Thee.

3 Onward we go, for still we hear them singing,
   "Come, weary souls, for Jesus bids you come;"
  And thro' the dark, its echoes sweetly ringing,
   The music of the Gospel leads us home.

129.

GUIDE me, O, Thou great Jehovah,
  Pilgrim thro' this barren land;
I am weak, but Thou art mighty;
  Hold me with Thy powerful hand:
Bread of heaven, Bread of heaven,
  Feed me till I want no more.

2 Open now the crystal fountain,
  Whence the healing waters flow;
Let the fiery, cloudy pillar
  Lead me all my journey thro':
Strong Deliverer, Strong Deliverer,
  Be Thou still my strength and shield.

3 When I tread the verge of Jordan,
  Bid my anxious fears subside;
Bear me through the swelling current,
  Land me safe on Canaan's side:
Songs of praises, Songs of praises,
  I will ever give to Thee.

130.

WE bow our knees unto the Father
  Of Christ the Lord of earth and heaven,

That riches of His grace and glory
  And pow'r for service may be given.
Cho.—We are waiting for the promise of the
      Father—
    For the Holy Spirit's power;
    O our Father, for Thy Spirit we are
      waiting, even now, this very hour.
  ‖: We are waiting for His coming, :‖
    For the Holy Spirit's power;
    O our Father, for Thy Spirit we are
      waiting, even now, this very hour.

2 O fill the inward man with power,
    As Christ within our hearts doth dwell;
  Our root in Him, tho' storms may lower,
    Victorious love we still shall tell.

3 The love that passeth knowledge give us,
    Its height and depth and breadth and
      length;
  Abundantly beyond our asking,
    Beyond our thought give us Thy strength.

4 Thy pow'r it is that worketh in us,
    O multiply it here to-day,
  And Christ, our Lord, shall have the glory
    Within His church through endless day.

131.

COME, praise the Lord, exalt His name,
    Our Saviour and our King;
  'Tis meet we should His praise proclaim,
    And hallelujah sing.

2 How great, how precious is His name,
    How poor the praise we bring;
  His people still should own His claim,
    And hallelujah sing.

3 A day will come, its dawn we greet,
    When heaven itself shall ring,

And all the saints with joy shall meet,
And hallelujah sing.

132.

SOMETIMES I catch sweet glimpses of
His face, But that is all;
Sometimes He looks on me and seems to
smile, But that is all;
Sometimes He speaks a passing word of
peace, But that is all;
Sometimes I think I hear His loving voice
Upon me call.

2 And is this all He meant when first He
said, "Come unto me"?
Is there no deeper, more enduring rest In
Him for thee?
Is there no steadier light for thee in Him?
O come and see;
Is there no deeper, more enduring rest In
Him for thee?

3 Nay, do not wrong Him by thy heavy
thoughts, But love His love;
Do thou full justice to His tenderness, His
mercy prove;
Take Him for what He is, O take Him all,
And look above;
And do not wrong Him by thy heavy
thoughts, But love His love.

4 Christ and His love shall be thy blessed all
For evermore;
Christ and His light shall shine on all thy
ways For evermore;
Christ and His peace shall keep thy
troubled soul For evermore;
Christ and His love shall be thy blessed all
For evermore.

133.

CHRISTIAN, walk *carefully*, danger is near;
On in thy journey with trembling and fear.
Snares from without and temptations within,
Seek to entice thee once more into sin.

Cho.—‖: Christian, walk *carefully*, :‖
    Christian, walk *carefully*,
        danger is near.

2 Christian, walk *cheerfully*, thro' the fierce storm,
Dark tho' the sky with its threat of alarm.
Soon will the clouds and the tempest be o'er,
Than with thy Saviour thou'lt rest evermore.

    ‖: Christian, walk *cheerfully*, :‖
    Christian, walk *cheerfully*
        through the fierce storm.

3 Christian, walk *pray'rfully*, oft wilt thou fall
If thou forget on thy Saviour to call;
Safe thou shall walk thro' each trial and care,
If thou art clad in the armor of pray'r.

    ‖: Christian, walk *pray'rfully*, :‖
    Christian, walk *pray'rfully*,
        fear lest thou fall.

4 Christian, walk *hopefully*, sorrow and pain
Cease when the haven of rest thou shalt gain;
Then from the lips of the Judge, thy reward:
"Enter thou into the joy of thy Lord."

    ‖: Christian, walk *hopefully*, :‖
    Christian, walk *hopefully*,
        rest thou shalt gain.

134.

He holds the key of all unknown,
 And I am glad;
If other hands should hold the key,
Or, if He trusted it to me,
I might be sad, I might be sad.

2 What if to-morrow's cares were here
Without its rest?
 I'd rather He unlocked the day,
 And as the hours swing open, say,
"My will is best," "My will is best."

3 The very dimness of my sight
Makes me secure;
 For, groping in my misty way,
 I feel His hand; I hear Him say,
"My help is sure," "My help is sure."

4 I cannot read His future plans,
But this I know:
 I have the smiling of His face,
 And all the refuge of His grace,
While here below, while here below.

5 Enough; this covers all my wants,
And so I rest;
 For, what I cannot, He can see,
 And, in His care I safe shall be,
Forever blest, forever blest.

135.

The cross it standeth fast,
 Hallelujah! hallelujah!
Defying ev'ry blast,
 Hallelujah! hallelujah!
The winds of hell have blown,
The world its hate hath shown,
Yet it is not overthrown,
 Hallelujah for the cross!

Cho.—‖: Hallelujah, hallelujah, hallelujah for
  the cross,
    Hallelujah, hallelujah, it shall never
      suffer loss. :‖

2 It is the old cross still,
    Hallelujah! hallelujah!
  Its triumph let us tell,
    Hallelujah! hallelujah!
  The grace of God here shone,
  Through Christ the blessed Son,
  Who did for sin atone,
    Hallelujah for the cross!

3 'Twas here the debt was paid,
    Hallelujah! hallelujah!
  Our sins on Jesus laid,
    Hallelujah! hallelujah!
  So round the cross we sing,
  Of Christ our offering,
  Of Christ our living King,
    Hallelujah for the cross!

136.

1 YOU'RE starting, my boy, on life's
    journey,
  Along the grand highway of life;
  You'll meet with a thousand temptations—
  Each city with evil is rife.
  This world is a stage of excitement,
    There is danger wherever you go;
  But if you are tempted in weakness,
    Have courage, my boy, to say No!

Cho.—‖: Have courage, my boy, to say No!:‖
  ‖: Have courage, my boy,:‖
    Have courage, my boy, to say No!

2 In courage alone lies your safety,
    When you the long journey begin;

Your trust in a heavenly Father
  Will keep you unspotted from sin.
Temptations will go on increasing,
  As streams from a rivulet flow;
But if you'd be true to your manhood,
  Have courage, my boy, to say No!

3 Be careful in choosing companions,
    Seek only the brave and the true;
  And stand by your friends when in trial,
    Ne'er changing the old for the new;
  And when by false friends you are tempted
    The taste of the wine cup to know,
  With firmness, with patience and kindness,
    Have courage, my boy, to say No!

137.

CHOOSE I must, and soon must choose
    Holiness, or heaven lose;
  While what heaven loves I hate,
  Shut for me is heaven's gate.

2 Endless sin means endless woe;
  Into endless sin I go,
  If my soul from reason rent,
  Takes from sin its final bent.

3 As the stream its channel grooves,
  And within that channel moves,
  So doth habit's deepest tide
  Groove its bed, and there abide.

4 Light obeyed increaseth light,
  Light resisted bringeth night;
  Who shall give me will to choose,
  If the love of light I lose?

5 Speed, my soul; this instant yield;
  Let the Light its sceptre wield;
  While thy God prolongeth grace,
  Haste thee toward His holy face!

138.

SOME day we say, and turn our eyes
  Toward the fair hills of Paradise;
Some day, some time, a sweet new rest
Shall blossom, flower-like, in each breast;
‖: Some day, some time, our eyes shall see
The faces kept in memory : ‖
Some day their hands shall clasp our hand,
‖: Just over in the morning land ; :‖
Some day their hands shall clasp our hand,
Just over in the morning land ;
O morning land! O morning land!

2 Some day our ears shall hear the song
Of triumph over sin and wrong;
Some day, some time, but oh! not yet;
But we will wait and not forget,
‖: That some day all these things shall be,
And rest be giv'n to you and me ; :‖
So wait, my friends, tho' years move slow,
‖: That happy time will come, we know ; :‖
So wait, my friends, tho' years move slow,
That happy time will come, we know,
O morning land! O morning land!

139.

COME to the Saviour, hear His loving
  voice,
  Never will you find a Friend so true;
Now He is waiting, trust Him and rejoice,
  Tenderly He calleth you.

CHO.—O, what a Saviour standing at the door,
  Haste while He lingers, pardon now
    implore;
  Still He is waiting, grieve His love no
    more,
  Tenderly He calleth you.

2 Blest words of comfort, gently now they
    fall,
  Jesus is the life, the truth, the way;

Come to the fountain, there is room for all,
  Jesus bids you come to-day.

3 Softly the Spirit whispers in the heart,
    Do not slight the Saviour's offered grace;
  Gladly receive Him, let Him not depart,
    Happy they who seek His face.

4 Light in the darkness, joy in any pain,
    Refuge for the weary and oppressed;
  Still He is waiting, calling yet again,
    Come and He will give you rest.

140.

O GOLDEN day, O day of God,
  When sinless souls the garden trod!
In bliss supreme, 'neath sunny skies,
In Eden fair, in Paradise.

Cho.—O Paradise, sweet Paradise,
    From scenes of earth we long to rise;
  O Paradise, bright Paradise,
    Where Jesus reigns beyond the skies.

2 The fatal fall, the sin, the shame,
  The death, the doom, the sword aflame,
  The curse, the crime beyond disguise,
  The earth no more is Paradise.

3 The beaded brow, the silvered hair,
  The aching heart, the vacant chair,
  The grassy graves, the broken ties,
  Are not the scenes of Paradise.

4 To Christ the Lord upon the tree,
  A sinner cries:—"Remember me!"
  "To-day shalt thou," the Lord replies,
  "Be with Me there in Paradise."

5 O golden day when Christ descends,
  The curse removes and sorrow ends;
  All glory clad, the ransomed rise
  To reign with Him in Paradise.

141.

I WILL sing the wond'rous story,
  Of the Christ who died for me,
How He left His home in glory,
  For the cross on Calvary.

Cho.—Yes, I'll sing the wondrous story
  Of the Christ who died for me,
Sing it with the saints in glory,
  Gathered by the crystal sea.

2 I was lost, but Jesus found me,
  Found the sheep that went astray;
Threw His loving arms around me,
  Drew me back into His way.

3 I was bruised, but Jesus healed me,
  Faint was I from many a fall,
Sight was gone, and fears possessed me,
  But He freed me from them all.

4 Days of darkness still come o'er me,
  Sorrow's paths I often tread,
But the Saviour still is with me,
  By His hand I'm safely led.

5 He will keep me till the river
  Rolls its waters at my feet;
Then He'll bear me safely over,
  Where the loved ones I shall meet.

142.

AWAKE, my soul, to joyful lays,
  And sing thy great Redeemer's praise;
He justly claims a song from me,
His loving-kindness, oh, how free!
Loving-kindness, loving-kindness,
His loving-kindness, oh, how free!

2 He saw me ruined in the fall,
  Yet loved me notwithstanding all;

He saved me from my lost estate,
His loving-kindness, oh, how great!
Loving-kindness, loving-kindness,
His loving-kindness, oh, how great!

3 Tho' num'rous hosts of mighty foes,
Tho' earth and hell my way oppose,
He safely leads my soul along,
His loving-kindness, oh, how strong!
Loving-kindness, loving-kindness,
His loving-kindness, oh, how strong!

4 When trouble, like a gloomy cloud,
Has gather'd thick, and thunder'd loud,
He near my soul has always stood,
His loving-kindness, oh, how good!
Loving-kindness, loving-kindness,
His loving-kindness, oh, how good!

143.

WELL, wife, I've found the model church,
  And worship'd there to-day;
It made me think of good old times,
  Before my hair was gray;
The meeting-house was finer built,
  Than they were years ago,
But then I found when I went in,
  It was not built for show.

2 The sexton did not set me down,
  Away back by the door;
He knew that I was old and deaf,
  And saw that I was poor;
He must have been a Christian man,
  He led me boldly through
The crowded aisle of that grand church,
  To find a pleasant pew.

3 I wish you'd heard the singing, wife,
  It had the old-time ring;

The preacher said with trumpet voice,
    Let all the people sing:
"Old Coronation," was the tune;
    The music upward roll'd,
Until I tho't the angel-choir
    Struck all their harps of gold.

4 My deafness seemed to melt away,
    My spirit caught the fire;
I joined my feeble, trembling voice
    With that melodious choir;
And sang as in my youthful days,
    "Let angels prostrate fall;
‖:Bring forth the royal diadem,
    And crown Him Lord of all.:‖

5 I tell you, wife, it did me good
    To sing that hymn once more:
I felt like some wrecked mariner
    Who gets a glimpse of shore;
I almost want to lay aside
    This weather-beaten form,
And anchor in the blessed port,
    Forever from the storm.

6 'Twas not a flowery sermon, wife,
    But simple gospel truth;
It fitted humble men like me;
    It suited hopeful youth;
To win immortal souls to Christ,
    The earnest preacher tried;
He talked not of himself, or creed,
    But Jesus crucified.

7 Dear wife, the toil will soon be o'er,
    The victory soon be won;
The shining land is just ahead,
    Our race is nearly run:
We're nearing Canaan's happy shore,
    Our home so bright and fair;

Thank God, we'll never sin again;
" ‖:There'll be no sorrow there,:‖
In heav'n above, Where all is love,
There'll be no sorrow there."

144.

THE Spirit and the bride say, "Come!
And take the water of life!"
O blessed call! Good news to all
Who tire of sin and strife.

Cho.—‖:The Spirit says, "Come!"
The bride says, "Come!"
And take of the water of life freely.:‖

2 Let ev'ry one who hears, say "Come!
And joyful witness give;"
I heard the sound, The stream I found,
I drank, and now I live!

3 Ye souls who are athirst, forsake
Your broken cisterns first;
Then come, partake, One draught will slake
Your soul's consuming thirst.

4 Yea, whosoever will may come,
Your longings Christ can fill;
The stream is free To you and me,
And whosoever will.

145.

WHILE Jesus whispers to you,
Come, sinner, come!
While we are praying for you,
Come, sinner, come!
Now is the time to own Him,
Come, sinner, come!
Now is the time to know Him,
Come, sinner, come!

2 Are you too heavy laden?
   Come, sinner, come!
Jesus will bear your burden,
   Come, sinner, come!
Jesus will not deceive you,
   Come, sinner, come!
Jesus can now redeem you,
   Come, sinner, come!

3 Oh, hear His tender pleading,
   Come, sinner, come!
Come and receive the blessing,
   Come, sinner, come!
While Jesus whispers to you,
   Come, sinner, come!
While we are praying for you,
   Come, sinner, come!

146.

WHEN the mists have rolled in splendor
   From the beauty of the hills,
And the sunlight falls in gladness,
   On the river and the rills,
We re-call our Father's promise
   In the rainbow of the spray:
We shall know each other better
   When the mists have rolled away.

Cho.—We shall know as we are known,
   Never more to walk alone,
In the dawning of the morning
   Of that bright and happy day:
We shall know each other better,
   When the mists have rolled away.

2 Oft we tread the path before us
   With a weary burden'd heart;
Oft we toil amid the shadows,
   And our fields are far apart:

But the Saviour's " Come, ye blessed,"
  All our labor will repay,
When we gather in the morning
  Where the mists have rolled away.

3 We shall come with joy and gladness,
  We shall gather round the throne;
Face to face with those that love us,
  We shall know as we are known:
And the song of our redemption,
  Shall resound thro' endless day,
When the shadows have departed,
  And the mists have rolled away.

147.

SAVIOUR, again to Thy dear name we raise
With one accord our parting hymn of praise;
Once more we bless Thee ere our worship cease,
Then, lowly kneeling, wait Thy word of peace.

2 Grant us Thy peace upon our homeward way;
With Thee begun, with Thee shall end the day;
Guard Thou the lips from sin, the hearts from shame,
That in this house have called upon Thy name.

3 Grant us Thy peace, Lord, thro' the coming night,
Turn Thou for us its darkness into light;
From harm and danger keep Thy children free,
For dark and light are both alike to Thee.

4 Grant us Thy peace throughout our earthly life,

Our balm in sorrow, and our stay in strife;
Then, when Thy voice shall bid our conflict cease,
Call us, O Lord, to Thine eternal peace.

18.

DOWN in the valley with my Saviour I would go,
Where the flow'rs are blooming and the sweet waters flow;
Ev'rywhere He leads me I would follow, follow on,
Walking in His footsteps till the crown be won.

EF.—Follow! follow! I would follow Jesus!
  Anywhere, ev'rywhere, I would follow on!
  Follow! follow! I would follow Jesus!
  Ev'rywhere, He leads me I would follow on!

Down in the valley with my Saviour I would go,
Where the storms are sweeping and the dark waters flow;
With His hand to lead me I will never, never fear,
Dangers cannot fright me if my Lord is near.

Down in the valley, or up on the mountain steep,
Close beside my Saviour would my soul ever keep;
He will lead me safely, in the path that He has trod,
Up to where they gather on the hills of God.

149.

Jesus knows thy sorrow,
　Knows thine ev'ry care;
Knows thy deep contrition,
　Hears thy feeblest prayer;
Do not fear to trust Him—
　Tell Him all thy grief;
Cast on Him thy burden,
　He will bring relief.

2 Trust the heart of Jesus,
　Thou art precious there;
Surely He would shield thee
　From the tempter's snare;
Safely He would lead thee
　By His own sweet way,
Out into the glory
　Of a brighter day.

3 Jesus knows thy conflict,
　Hears thy burdened sigh;
When thy heart is wounded,
　Hears the plaintive cry;
He thy soul will strengthen,
　Overcome thy fears;
He will send thee comfort,
　Wipe away thy tears.

150.

Gather them in! for yet there is room
　At the feast that the King has spread;
Oh, gather them in! let His house be filled,
　And the hungry and poor be fed.

Ref.—Out in the highway, out in the byway,
　Out in the dark paths of sin,
Go forth, go forth, with a loving heart,
　And gather the wand'rers in!

2 Gather them in! for yet there is room;
But our hearts—how they throb with pain,
To think of the many who slight the call
That may never be heard again!

3 Gather them in! for yet there is room;
'Tis a message from God above;
Oh, gather them into the fold of grace,
And the arms of the Saviour's love!

151.
COME, we that love the Lord,
And let your joys be known,
‖:Join in a song with sweet accord,:‖
‖: And thus surround the throne. :‖

Cho.—We're marching to Zion,
Beautiful, beautiful Zion;
We're marching upward to Zion,
The beautiful city of God.

2 Let those refuse to sing
Who never knew our God;
‖: But children of the heav'nly King,:‖
‖: May speak their joys abroad. :‖

3 The hill of Zion yields
A thousand sacred sweets,
‖: Before we reach the heav'nly fields, :‖
‖: Or walk the golden streets. :‖

4 Then let our songs abound,
And ev'ry tear be dry;
‖: We're marching thro' Immanuel's ground,:‖
‖: To fairer worlds on high. :‖

152.
HAVE you any room for Jesus,
He who bore your load of sin;
As He knocks and asks admission,
Sinner will you let Him in?

Cho.—Room for Jesus, King of glory,
  Hasten now His word obey,
 Swing the heart's door widely open,
  Bid Him enter while you may.

2 Room for pleasure, room for business,
  But for Christ the crucified;
 Not a place that He can enter,
  In your heart for which He died?

3 Have you any room for Jesus,
  As in grace He calls again?
 O to-day is time accepted,
  To-morrow you may call in vain.

4 Room and time now give to Jesus,
  Soon will pass God's day of grace;
 Soon thy heart left cold and silent,
  And thy Saviour's pleading cease.

153.

"Almost persuaded," Now to believe;
 "Almost persuaded," Christ to receive;
  Seems now some soul to say,
  "Go, Spirit, go Thy way,
  Some more convenient day
   On Thee I'll call."

2 "Almost persuaded," Come, come to-day;
 "Almost persuaded," Turn not away·
  Jesus invites you here,
  Angels are lingering near,
  Prayers rise from hearts so dear:
   "O wanderer, come."

3 "Almost persuaded," Harvest is past!
 "Almost persuaded," Doom comes at last!
  "Almost" cannot avail;
  "Almost" is but to fail!
  Sad, sad, that bitter wail—
   "Almost—*but lost!*"

154.

There were ninety and nine that safely lay
　In the shelter of the fold,
But one was out on the hills away,
　Far off from the gates of gold—
Away on the mountains wild and bare,
‖: Away from the tender Shepherd's care.:‖

2 " Lord, Thou hast here Thy ninety and nine:
　Are they not enough for Thee?"
But the Shepherd made answer: " This of mine
　Has wandered away from me,
And, although the road be rough and steep
‖: I go to the desert to find my sheep.":‖

3 But none of the ransomed ever knew
　How deep were the waters cross'd;
Nor how dark was the night that the Lord pass'd thro'
　Ere He found His sheep that was lost.
Out in the desert He heard its cry—
‖: Sick and helpless, and ready to die.:‖

4 " Lord, whence are those blood-drops all the way
　That mark out the mountain's track?"
" They were shed for one who had gone astray
　Ere the Shepherd could bring him back,"
" Lord, whence are Thy hands so rent and torn?"
　‖: They are pierced to-night by many a thorn.":‖

5 But all thro' the mountains, thunder-riven,
　And up from the rocky steep,
There rose a glad cry to the gate of heaven,
　" Rejoice! I have found my sheep!"

And the angels echoed around the throne,
‖: "Rejoice, for the Lord brings back His
own!":‖

155.

REVIVE Thy work, O Lord!
  Thy mighty arm make bare;
Speak with the voice that wakes the dead,
  And make Thy people hear.

Cho.—Revive (Thy work)! revive (Thy
    work)!
  And give refreshing showers;
The glory shall be all Thine own;
  The blessing shall be ours.

2 Revive Thy work, O Lord!
  Disturb this sleep of death;
Quicken the smould'ring embers now
  By Thine Almighty breath.

3 Revive Thy work, O Lord!
  Create soul-thirst for Thee;
But hung'ring for the bread of life,
  Oh, may our spirits be!

4 Revive Thy work, O Lord!
  Exalt Thy precious name;
And, by the Holy Ghost, our love
  For Thee and Thine inflame.

156.

I AM Thine, O Lord, I have heard Thy
  voice,
  And it told Thy love to me;
But I long to rise in the arms of faith,
  And be closer drawn to Thee.

Ref.—Draw me nearer, nearer, blessed Lord,
    To the cross where Thou hast died;
  Draw me nearer, nearer, nearer, bles-
    sed Lord,
    To Thy precious, bleeding side.

2 Consecrate me now to Thy service, Lord,
　　By the pow'r of grace divine;
　Let my soul look up with a steadfast hope,
　　And my will be lost in Thine.

3 O the pure delight of a single hour
　　That before Thy throne I spend,
　When I kneel in pray'r, and with Thee,
　　my God,
　I commune as friend with friend.

4 There are depths of love that I cannot
　　know
　　Till I cross the narrow sea,
　There are heights of joy that I may not
　　reach
　　Till I rest in peace with Thee.

157.

WHEN peace, like a river, attendeth
　　my way,
　When sorrows like sea-billows roll;
　Whatever my lot, Thou hast taught me to
　　say,
　　It is well, it is well with my soul.

Cho.—It is well with my soul,
　　It is well, it is well with my soul.

2 Though Satan should buffet, though trials
　　should come,
　　Let this blest assurance control,
　That Christ hath regarded my helpless
　　estate,
　　And hath shed His own blood for my
　　soul.

3 My sin—oh, the bliss of this glorious
　　thought—
　　My sin—not in part but the whole,

Is nailed to His cross and I bear it no more,
  Praise the Lord, praise the Lord, oh, my soul!

4 And, Lord, haste the day when the faith shall be sight,
  The clouds be rolled back as a scroll,
  The trump shall resound, and the Lord shall descend,
  " Even so "—it is well with my soul.

158.

O SAFE to the Rock that is higher than I,
  My soul in its conflicts and sorrows would fly;
  So sinful, so weary, Thine, Thine would I be;
  Thou blest " Rock of Ages," I'm hiding in Thee.

Cho.—Hiding in Thee, hiding in Thee,
  Thou blest " Rock of Ages,"
  I'm hiding in Thee.

2 In the calm of the noontide, in sorrow's lone hour,
  In times when temptation casts o'er me its power;
  In the tempests of life, on its wide, heaving sea,
  Thou blest " Rock of Ages," I'm hiding in Thee.

3 How oft in the conflict, when pressed by the foe,
  I have fled to my Refuge and breathed out my woe;
  How often when trials, like sea-billows roll,
  Have I hidden in Thee, O Thou Rock of my soul.

159.

Oh, where are the reapers that garner in
  The sheaves of the good from the fields of sin;
With sickles of truth must the work be done,
And no one may rest till the "harvest home."

Cho.—Where are the reapers? Oh, who will come
    And share in the glory of the "harvest home?"
  Oh, who will help us to garner in
  The sheaves of good from the fields of sin.

2 Go out in the by-ways and search them all;
  The wheat may be there, though the weeds are tall;
  Then search in the highway, and pass none by,
  But gather from all for the home on high.

3 The fields all are ripening, and far and wide
  The world now is waiting the harvest tide;
  But reapers are few, and the work is great,
  And much will be lost should the harvest wait.

4 So come with your sickles, ye sons of men,
  And gather together the golden grain;
  Toil on till the Lord of the harvest come,
  Then share ye His joy in the "harvest home."

160.

To the work! to the work! we are servants of God,
  Let us follow the path that our Master has trod;

With the balm of His counsel our strength
    to renew,
Let us do with our might what our hands
    find to do.

Cho.—‖: Toiling on, toiling on,:‖
    Let us hope, let us watch,
    And labor till the Master comes.

2 To the work! to the work! let the hungry
    be fed;
To the fountain of life let the weary be led;
In the cross and its banner our glory shall
    be,
While we herald the tidings, "*Salvation is
    free!*"

3 To the work! to the work! there is labor
    for all,
For the kingdom of darkness and error
    shall fall;
And the name of Jehovah exalted shall be
In the loud swelling chorus, "*Salvation is
    free!*"

4 To the work! to the work! in the strength
    of the Lord,
And a robe and a crown shall our labor re-
    ward;
When the home of the faithful our dwell-
    ing shall be,
And we shout with the ransomed, "*Salva-
    tion is free!*"

161.

I WILL sing of my Redeemer
    And His wondrous love to me;
On the cruel cross He suffered,
    From the curse to set me free.

Cho.—Sing, oh! sing, of my Redeemer,
　　With His blood He purchased me,
　On the cross He sealed my pardon,
　　Paid the debt, and made me free.

2 I will tell the wondrous story,
　　How my lost estate to save,
　In His boundless love and mercy,
　　He the ransom freely gave.

3 I will praise my dear Redeemer,
　　His triumphant power I'll tell,
　How the victory He giveth
　　Over sin, and death, and hell.

4 I will sing of my Redeemer,
　　And His heavenly love to me;
　He from death to life hath brought me,
　　Son of God, with Him to be.

162.

THERE are lonely hearts to cherish,
　　While the days are going by;
There are weary souls who perish,
　　While the days are going by;
If a smile we can renew,
　As our journey we pursue,
Oh, the good we all may do,
　While the days are going by.

Ref.—Going by, going by,
　　Going by, going by,
　　Oh, the good we all may do,
　　While the days are going by.

2 There's no time for idle scorning,
　　While the days are going by;
　Let your face be like the morning,
　　While the days are going by;
　Oh, the world is full of sighs,
　　Full of sad and weeping eyes;

Help your fallen brother rise,
  While the days are going by.

3 All the loving links that bind us,
  While the days are going by ;
One by one we leave behind us,
  While the days are going by ;
But the seeds of good we sow,
  Both in shade and shine will grow,
And will keep our hearts aglow,
  While the days are going by.

163.

SING them over again to me,
  Wonderful words of Life,
Let me more of their beauty see,
  Wonderful words of Life.
Words of life and beauty,
  Teach me faith and duty ;
‖: Beautiful words, wonderful words,
  Wonderful words of Life.:‖

2 Christ, the blessed One, gives to all
  Wonderful words of Life,
Sinner, list to the loving call,
  Wonderful words of Life.
All so freely given,
  Wooing us to heaven.
‖: Beautiful words, wonderful words,
  Wonderful words of Life.:‖

3 Sweetly echo the gospel call,
  Wonderful words of Life,
Offer pardon and peace to all,
  Wonderful words of Life.
Jesus, only Saviour,
  Sanctify forever.
‖: Beautiful words, wonderful words,
  Wonderful words of Life :‖

164.

Behold, what love, what boundless love,
　The Father hath bestowed
On sinners lost, that we should be
　Now called the sons of God!

Cho.—Behold, what manner of love!
　　What manner of love the Father hath
　　　bestowed upon us,
　　That we—that we should be call'd,
　　Should be call'd the sons of God.

2 No longer far from Him, but now
　By "precious blood" made nigh;
Accepted in the "Well-beloved,"
　Near to God's heart we lie.

3 What we in glory soon shall be,
　It doth not yet appear;
But when our precious Lord we see,
　We shall His image bear.

4 With such a blessed hope in view,
　We would more holy be,
More like our risen, glorious Lord,
　Whose face we soon shall see.

165.

Simply trusting every day,
　Trusting through a stormy way;
Even when my faith is small,
Trusting Jesus, that is all.

Cho.—Trusting as the moments fly,
　　Trusting as the days go by;
　　Trusting Him whate'er befall,
　　Trusting Jesus, that is all.

2 Brightly doth His Spirit shine
　Into this poor heart of mine;

While He leads I cannot fall,
　　　Trusting Jesus, that is all.

　　3 Singing, if my way is clear;
　　　Praying if the path is drear;
　　　If in danger, for Him call;
　　　Trusting Jesus, that is all.

　　4 Trusting Him while life shall last,
　　　Trusting Him till earth is past;
　　　Till within the jasper wall,
　　　Trusting Jesus, that is all.

166.

YIELD not to temptation
　　For yielding is sin,
Each vict'ry will help you
　　Some other to win;
Fight manfully onward,
　　Dark passions subdue,
Look ever to Jesus,
　　He'll carry you through.

Cho.—Ask the Saviour to help you,
　　　Comfort, strengthen, and keep you;
　　He is willing to aid you,
　　　He wll carry you through.

2 Shun evil companions,
　　Bad language disdain,
God's name hold in rev'rence,
　　Nor take it in vain;
Be thoughtful and earnest,
　　Kind-hearted and true,
Look ever to Jesus,
　　He'll carry you through.

3 To him that o'ercometh
　　God giveth a crown,
Thro' faith we shall conquer,
　　Though often cast down;

He who is our Saviour,
  Our strength will renew,
Look ever to Jesus,
  He'll carry you through.

167.

WHAT a friend we have in Jesus,
  All our sins and griefs to bear;
What a privilege to carry
  Everything to God in prayer.
Oh, what piece we often forfeit,
  Oh, what needless pain we bear—
All because we do not carry
  Everything to God in prayer.

2 Have we trials and temptations?
  Is there trouble anywhere?
We should never be discouraged,
  Take it to the Lord in prayer.
Can we find a Friend so faithful,
  Who will all our sorrows share?
Jesus knows our every weakness,
  Take it to the Lord in prayer.

3 Are we weak and heavy laden,
  Cumbered with a load of care?
Precious Saviour, still our Refuge,—
  Take it to the Lord in prayer.
Do thy friends despise, forsake thee?
  Take it to the Lord in prayer;
In His arms He'll take and shield thee,
  Thou wilt find a solace there.

168.

I'VE found a Friend; oh, such a Friend!
  He loved me ere I knew Him;
He drew me with the cords of love,
  And thus He bound me to Him.
And 'round my heart still closely twine
  Those ties which naught can sever,

For I am His, and He is mine,
 Forever and forever.

2 I've found a Friend; oh, such a Friend!
 He bled, He died to save me;
And not alone the gift of life,
 But His own self He gave me.
Naught that I have my own I call,
 I hold it for the Giver:
My heart, my strength, my life, my all,
 Are His, and His forever.

3 I've found a Friend; oh, such a Friend!
 All power to Him is given;
To guard me on my onward course,
 And bring me safe to heaven.
Th' eternal glories gleam afar,
 To nerve my faint endeavor:
So now to watch, to work, to war,
 And then to rest forever.

4 I've found a Friend; oh, such a Friend!
 So kind, and true, and tender,
So wise a Counsellor and Guide,
 So mighty a Defender!
From Him, who loves me now so well,
 What power my soul can sever?
Shall life or death, or earth or hell?
 No; I am His forever.

169.

PASS me not, O gentle Saviour,
 Hear my humble cry;
While on others Thou art smiling,
 Do not pass me by.

Cho.—Saviour, Saviour,
 Hear my humble cry,
 While on others Thou art calling,
 Do not pass me by.

2 Let me at a throne of mercy
    Find a sweet relief ;
Kneeling there in deep contrition,
    Help my unbelief:

3 Trusting only in Thy merit,
    Would I seek Thy face ;
Heal my wounded, broken spirit,
    Save me by Thy grace.

4 Thou the Spring of all my comfort
    More than life to me,
Whom have I on earth beside Thee ?
    Whom in heaven but Thee ?

170.

MY Jesus, I love Thee, I know Thou art mine,
For Thee all the follies of sin I resign ;
My gracious Redeemer, my Saviour art Thou,
If ever I loved Thee, my Jesus, 'tis now.

2 I love Thee, because Thou hast first loved me,
And purchased my pardon on Calvary's tree ;
I love Thee for wearing the thorns on Thy brow ;
If ever I loved Thee, my Jesus, 'tis now.

3 I will love Thee in life, I will love Thee in death,
And praise Thee as long as Thou lendest me breath ;
And say when the death-dew lies cold on my brow,
If ever I loved Thee, my Jesus, 'tis now.

4 In mansions of glory and endless delight,
I'll ever adore Thee in heaven so bright;

I'll sing with the glittering crown on my
 brow,
If ever I loved Thee, my Jesus, 'tis now.

171.

1 COME, ev'ry soul by sin oppressed,
   There's mercy with the Lord,
And He will surely give you rest,
   By trusting in His word.

Cho.—Only trust Him, only trust Him,
   Only trust Him, now;
He will save you, He will save you,
   He will save you now.

2 For Jesus shed His precious blood
   Rich blessings to bestow;
Plunge now into the crimson flood
   That washes white as snow.

3 Yes, Jesus is the Truth, the Way,
   That leads you into rest;
Believe in Him without delay,
   And you are fully blest.

4 Come then, and join this holy band,
   And on to glory go,
To dwell in that celestial land,
   Where joys immortal flow.

172.

1 I HEAR the Saviour say,
   Thy strength indeed is small;
Child of weakness, watch and pray,
   Find in Me thine all in all.

Cho.—Jesus, paid it all,
   All to Him I owe;
Sin had left a crimson stain;
   He washed it white as snow.

2 Lord, now indeed I find
  Thy pow'r, and that alone,
Can change the leper's spots,
  And melt the heart of stone.

3 For nothing good have I
  Whereby Thy grace to claim—
I'll wash my garments white
  In the blood of Calvary's Lamb.

4 When from my dying bed
  My ransomed soul shall rise,
Then "Jesus paid it all"
  Shall rend the vaulted skies.

5 And when before the throne
  I stand in Him complete,
I'll lay my trophies down,
  All down at Jesus' feet.

173.

I HAVE a Saviour, He's pleading in glory,
  A dear, loving Saviour, tho' earth-friends be few;
And now He is watching in tenderness o'er me,
  And oh, that my Saviour were your Saviour too.

Cho.—For you I am praying,
  For you I am praying,
  For you I am praying,
    I'm praying for you.

2 I have a Father: to me He has given
  A hope for eternity, blessed and true:
And soon will He call me to meet Him in heaven,
  But oh, that He'd let me bring you with me too

3 I have a robe: 'tis resplendent in whiteness,
   Awaiting in glory my wondering view;
Oh, when I receive it all shining in brightness,
   Dear friends, could I see you receiving one too!

4 I have a peace: it is calm as a river—
   A peace that the friends of this world never knew;
My Saviour alone is its Author and Giver,
   And oh, could I know it was given to you!
When Jesus has found you, tell others the story,
   That my loving Saviour is your Saviour too;
Then pray that your Saviour may bring them to glory,
   And pray'r will be answered—'twas answered for you!

174.

SOUL of mine, in earthly temple,
   Why not here content abide?
Why art thou forever pleading?
   Why art thou not satisfied?

Cho.—‖: I shall be satisfied,
   I shall be satisfied,
     When I awake in His likeness.:‖

2 Soul of mine, my heart is clinging
   To the earth's fair pomp and pride;
Ah, why dost thou thus reprove me?
   Why art thou not satisfied?

3 Soul of mine, must I surrender,
   See myself as crucified;
Turn from all of earth's ambition,
   That thou mayest be satisfied?

4 Soul of mine, continue pleading;
   Sin rebuke, and folly chide;
I accept the cross of Jesus,
   That thou mayest be satisfied.

175.

SAVIOUR! Thy dying love
   Thou gavest me,
Nor should I aught withhold,
   Dear Lord, from Thee;
In love my soul would bow,
   My heart fulfill its vow,
Some offering bring Thee now,
   Something for Thee.

2 O'er the blest mercy-seat,
   Pleading for me,
My feeble faith looks up,
   Jesus, to Thee:
Help me the cross to bear,
   Thy wondrous love declare,
Some song to raise, or prayer,
   Something for Thee.

3 Give me a faithful heart—
   Likeness to Thee—
That each departing day
   Henceforth may see
Some work of love begun,
   Some deed of kindness done,
Some wand'rer sought and won,
   Something for Thee.

4 All that I am and have—
   Thy gifts so free—
In joy, in grief, through life,
   Dear Lord, for Thee!
And when Thy face I see,
   My ransomed soul shall be,
Through all eternity,
   Something for Thee.

176.

Rescue the perishing,
  Care for the dying,
Snatch them in pity from sin and the grave;
  Weep o'er the erring one,
  Lift up the fallen,
Tell them of Jesus, the mighty to save.

Cho.—Rescue the perishing,
    Care for the dying;
    Jesus is merciful,
    Jesus will save.

2 Though they are slighting Him,
    Still He is waiting,
  Waiting the penitent child to receive.
    Plead with them earnestly,
    Plead with them gently:
  He will forgive if they only believe.

3 Down in the human heart,
    Crushed by the tempter,
  Feelings lie buried that grace can restore:
    Touched by a loving heart,
    Wakened by kindness,
  Chords that were broken will vibrate once more.

4 Rescue the perishing,
    Duty demands it;
  Strength for thy labor the Lord will provide:
    Back to the narrow way
    Patiently win them;
  Tell the poor wanderer a Saviour has died.

177.

Saviour, more than life to me,
  I am clinging, clinging close to Thee;
Let Thy precious blood applied,
Keep me ever, ever near Thy side.

Ref.—Every day, every hour,
 Let me feel Thy cleansing pow'r;
 May Thy tender love to me
 Bind me closer, closer, Lord, to Thee.

2 Thro' this changing world below,
 Lead me gently, gently as I go;
 Trusting Thee, I cannot stray,
 I can never, never lose my way.

3 Let me love Thee more and more,
 Till this fleeting, fleeting life is o'er;
 Till my soul is lost in love,
 In a brighter, brighter world above.

178.

MORE holiness give me,
 More strivings within;
More patience in suffering,
 More sorrow for sin;
More faith in my Saviour,
 More sense of His care;
More joy in His service,
 More purpose in prayer.

2 More gratitude give me,
 More trust in the Lord;
More pride in His glory,
 More hope in His word;
More tears for His sorrows,
 More pain at His grief;
More meekness in trial,
 More praise for relief.

3 More purity give me,
 More strength to o'ercome;
More freedom from earth-stains,
 More longings for home;
More fit for the kingdom,
 More used would I be;

More blessed and holy,
More, Saviour, *like Thee.*

179.

I HEAR Thy welcome voice
That calls me, Lord, to Thee
For cleansing in Thy precious blood
That flow'd on Calvary.

Cho.—I am coming, Lord!
Coming now to Thee!
Wash me, cleanse me, in the blood
That flow'd on Calvary.

2 Tho' coming weak and vile,
Thou dost my strength assure;
Thou dost my vileness fully cleanse,
Till spotless all and pure.

3 'Tis Jesus calls me on
To perfect faith and love,
To perfect hope, and peace, and trust,
For earth and heav'n above.

4 'Tis Jesus who confirms
The blessed work within,
By adding grace to welcomed grace,
Where reigned the power of sin.

5 And He the witness gives
To loyal hearts and free,
That every promise is fulfilled,
If faith but brings the plea.

6 All hail, atoning blood!
All hail, redeeming grace!
All hail, the Gift of Christ, our Lord,
Our Strength and Righteousness!

180.

'TIS the blessed hour of prayer, when
our hearts lowly bend,

And we gather to Jesus, our Saviour and Friend;
If we come to Him in faith, His protection to share,
What a balm for the weary! O how sweet to be there!

Cho.—‖: Blessed hour of pray'r, Blessed hour of pray'r,
What a balm for the weary! O how sweet to be there!:‖

2 'Tis the blessed hour of prayer, when the Saviour draws near,
With a tender compassion His children to hear;
When He tells us we may cast at His feet every care;
What a balm for the weary! O how sweet to be there!

3 'Tis the blessed hour of prayer, when the tempted and tried
To the Saviour who loves them their sorrow confide;
With a sympathizing heart He removes ev'ry care;
What a balm for the weary! O how sweet to be there!

4 At the blessed hour of prayer, trusting Him to believe
That the blessings we're needing we'll surely receive,
In the fullness of this trust we shall lose ev'ry care;
What a balm for the weary! O how sweet to be there!

181.

I NEED Thee ev'ry hour,
  Most gracious Lord;
No tender voice like Thine
  Can peace afford.

Ref.—I need Thee, oh! I need Thee
  Ev'ry hour I need Thee;
  O bless me now, my Saviour!
  I come to Thee.

2 I need Thee ev'ry hour;
  Stay Thou near by;
Temptations lose their pow'r
  When Thou art nigh.

3 I need Thee ev'ry hour,
  In joy or pain;
Come quickly and abide,
  Or life is vain.

4 I need Thee ev'ry hour;
  Teach me Thy will;
And Thy rich promises
  In me fulfill.

5 I need Thee ev'ry hour,
  Most Holy One;
Oh, make me Thine indeed,
  Thou blessèd Son.

182.

JESUS, keep me near the Cross,
  There a precious fountain
Free to all—a healing stream,
  Flows from Calvary's mountain

Cho.—In the Cross, in the Cross,
  Be my glory ever;
  Till my raptured soul shall find
  Rest beyond the river.

2 Near the Cross, a trembling soul,
   Love and mercy found me;
There the Bright and Morning Star
   Shed its beams around me.

3 Near the Cross! O Lamb of God,
   Bring its scenes before me;
Help me walk from day to day,
   With its shadows o'er me.

4 Near the Cross I'll watch and wait,
   Hoping, trusting ever,
Till I reach the golden strand,
   Just beyond the river.

183.

THOU my everlasting portion,
   More than friend or life to me,
All along my pilgrim journey,
   Saviour, let me walk with Thee.

REF.—Close to Thee, close to Thee,
   Close to Thee, close to Thee;
All along my pilgrim journey,
   Saviour, let me walk with Thee.

Not for ease or worldly pleasure,
   Nor for fame my prayer shall be;
Gladly will I toil and suffer,
   Only let me walk with Thee.

REF.—Close to Thee, close to Thee,
   Close to Thee, close to Thee;
Gladly will I toil and suffer,
   Only let me walk with Thee.

3 Lead me thro' the vale of shadows,
   Bear me o'er life's fitful sea;
Then the gate of life eternal,
   May I enter, Lord, with Thee.

Ref.—Close to Thee, close to Thee,
Close to Thee, close to Thee;
Then the gate of life eternal,
May I enter, Lord, with Thee.

184.

I GAVE My life for thee,
My precious blood I shed,
That thou might'st ransomed be,
And quickened from the dead;
I gave, I gave My life for thee,
What hast thou given for Me?

2 My Father's house of light,—
My glory-circled throne
I left, for earthly night,
For wand'rings sad and lone;
I left, I left it all for thee.
Hast thou left aught for Me?

3 I suffered much for thee,
More than thy tongue can tell,
Of bitterest agony,
To rescue thee from hell;
I've borne, I've borne it all for thee,
What hast thou borne for Me?

4 And I have brought to thee,
Down from My home above,
Salvation full and free,
My pardon and My love;
I bring, I bring rich gifts to thee,
What hast thou brought to Me?

185.

THERE is a green hill far away,
Without a city wall;
Where the dear Lord was crucified,
Who died to save us all.

Cho.—Oh dearly, dearly has He loved,
And we must love Him too;
And trust in His redeeming blood,
And try His works to do.

2 We may not know, we cannot tell
What pains He had to bear;
But we believe it was for us
He hung and suffered there.

3 He died that we might be forgiven,
He died to make us good,
That we might go at last to heav'n,
Saved by His precious blood.

4 There was no other good enough,
To pay the price of sin;
He only could unlock the gate
Of heav'n and let us in.

186.

BEYOND the smiling and the weeping,
I shall be soon, I shall be soon;
Beyond the waking and the sleeping,
Beyond the sowing and the reaping,
I shall be soon, I shall be soon.

Ref.—Love, rest and home!
Sweet, sweet home!
Lord, tarry not,
Lord, tarry not, but come.

2 Beyond the blooming and the fading,
I shall be soon, I shall be soon;
Beyond the shining and the shading,
Beyond the hoping and the dreading,
I shall be soon, I shall be soon.

3 Beyond the parting and the meeting,
I shall be soon, I shall be soon;
Beyond the farewell and the greeting,

Beyond the pulse's fever beating,
 I shall be soon, I shall be soon.

4 Beyond the frost-chain and the fever,
 I shall be soon, I shall be soon;
 Beyond the rock-waste and the river,
 Beyond the ever and the never,
 I shall be soon, I shall be soon.

187.

OH, the clanging bells of Time!
 Night and day they never cease;
We are wearied with their chime,
 For they do not bring us peace;
And we hush our breath to hear,
 And we strain our eyes to see
If thy shores are drawing near,—
 Eternity! Eternity!

2 Oh, the clanging bells of Time!
 How their changes rise and fall,
But in undertone sublime,
 Sounding clearly through them all,
Is a voice that must be heard,
 As our moments onward flee,
And it speaketh, aye, one word,—
 Eternity! Eternity!

3 Oh, the clanging bells of Time!
 To their voices, loud and low,
In a long, unresting line,
 We are marching to and fro;
And we yearn for sight or sound,
 Of the life that is to be,
For thy breath doth wrap us round,—
 Eternity! Eternity!

4 Oh, the clanging bells of Time!
 Soon their notes will all be dumb,

And in joy and peace sublime,
  We shall feel the silence come;
And our souls their thirst will slake,
  And our eyes the King will see,
When thy glorious morn shall break—
  Eternity! Eternity!

188.

WE shall meet beyond the river,
  By and by, by and by;
And the darkness shall be over,
  By and by, by and by;
With the toilsome journey done,
And the glorious battle won,
We shall shine forth as the sun,
  By and by, by and by.

2 We shall strike the harps of glory,
  By and by, by and by;
We shall sing redemption's story,
  By and by, by and by;
And the strains for evermore
Shall resound in sweetness o'er
Yonder everlasting shore,
  By and by, by and by.

3 We shall see and be like Jesus,
  By and by, by and by;
Who a crown of life will give us,
  By and by, by and by;
And the angels who fulfill
All the mandates of His will
Shall attend, and love us still,
  By and by, by and by.

4 There our tears shall all cease flowing,
  By and by, by and by;
And with sweetest rapture knowing,
  By and by, by and by;

All the blest ones, who have gone
To the land of life and song,—
We with shoutings shall rejoin,
  By and by, by and by.

189.

CHRIST is coming! let creation
  From her groans and travail cease;
Let the glorious proclamation
  Hope restore and faith increase:

Cho.—Christ is coming! Christ is coming!
    Come, Thou blessed Prince of peace!
  Christ is coming! Christ is coming!
    Come, Thou blessed Prince of peace!

2 Earth can now but tell the story
  Of Thy bitter cross and pain;
She shall yet behold Thy glory,
  When Thou comest back to reign.

3 Though once cradled in a manger,
  Oft no pillow but the sod;
Here an alien and a stranger,
  Mock'd of men, disown'd of God.

4 Long Thy exiles have been pining,
  Far from rest, and home, and Thee;
But, in heavenly vesture shining,
  Soon they shall Thy glory see.

5 With that "blessed hope" before us,
  Let no harp remain unstrung;
Let the mighty ransom'd chorus
  Onward roll from tongue to tongue.

190.

JOY to the world! the Lord is come;
  Let earth receive her King;

Let ev'ry heart prepare Him room,
   And heav'n and nature sing.

Joy to the world! the Saviour reigns;
   Let men their songs employ;
While fields and floods, rocks, hills, and
     plains,
   Repeat the sounding joy.

He rules the world with truth and grace,
   And makes the nations prove
The glories of His righteousness,
   And wonders of His love.

91.

I AM far frae my hame, an' I'm weary aften-whiles,
For the langed-for hame-bringin', an' my Father's welcome smiles,
An' I'll ne'er be fu' content, until mine een do see
The gowden gates o' heav'n an' my ain countrie.

The earth is fleck'd wi' flowers, mony-tinted, fresh an' gay,
The birdies warble blithely, for my Faither made them sae:
But these sights an' these soun's will as naething be to me,
When I hear the angels singin' in my ain countrie.

I've His gude word o' promise that some gladsome day, the King
To His ain royal palace His banished hame will bring;
Wi' een an' wi' hert rinnin ower, we shall see
The King in His beauty, in oor ain countrie.

My sins hae been mony, an' my sorrows
   hae been sair,
But there they'll never vex me, nor be remembered mair
For His bluid has made me white, and His
   han' shall dry my e'e,
When He brings me hame at last, to my
   ain countrie.

3 Sae little noo I ken, o' yon blessed, bonnie
   place,
I only ken it's Hame, whaur we shall see
   His face;
It wad surely be eneuch for ever mair to be
In the glory o' His presence, in oor ain
   countrie.
Like a bairn to his mither, a wee birdie to
   its nest,
I wad fain be gangin' noo, unto my Saviour's breast,
For He gathers in His bosom witless,
   worthless lambs like me,
An' carries them Himsel', to His ain
   countrie.

4 He is faithfu' that hath promised, an' He'll
   surely come again,
He'll keep His tryst wi' me, at what hour
   I dinna ken;
But He bids me still to wait, an' ready aye
   to be,
To gang at ony moment to my ain countrie.
Sae I'm watching aye, an' singin' o' my
   hame as I wait
For the soun'ing o' His footfa' this side the
   gowden gate:
God gie His grace to ilka ane wha' listens
   noo to me,
That we a' may gang in gladness to oor ain
   countrie.

192.

I'VE reached the land of corn and wine,
And all its riches freely mine;
Here shines undimm'd one blissful day,
For all my night has passed away.

Cho.—O Beulah land, sweet Beulah land,
As on thy highest mount I stand,
I look away across the sea,
Where mansions are prepared for me,
And view the shining glory shore,
My heav'n, my home for evermore.

2 The Saviour comes and walks with me,
And sweet communion here have we;
He gently leads me with His hand,
For this is heaven's border-land.

3 A sweet perfume upon the breeze
Is borne from ever vernal trees,
And flowers that never fading grow
Where streams of life forever flow.

4 The zephyrs seem to float to me,
Sweet sounds of heaven's melody,
As angels, with the white robed throng,
Join in the sweet redemption song.

193.

SOWING in the morning, sowing seeds of kindness,
Sowing in the noontide and the dewy eve;
Waiting for the harvest, and the time of reaping,
We shall come rejoicing, bringing in the sheaves.

Cho.—‖: Bringing in the sheaves,
Bringing in the sheaves,
We shall come rejoicing,
Bringing in the sheaves. :‖

2 Sowing in the sunshine, sowing in the
    shadows,
  Fearing neither clouds nor winter's chil-
      ling breeze;
 By and by the harvest, and the labor
    ended,
  We shall come, rejoicing, bringing in the
      sheaves.

3 Going forth with weeping, sowing for the
    Master,
  Tho' the loss sustain'd our spirit often
      grieves;
 When our weeping's over, He will bid us
    welcome,
  We shall come, rejoicing, bringing in the
      sheaves.

194.

DEPTH of mercy! can it be
    Mercy still reserved for me?
Can my God His wrath forbear?
‖: Me, the chief of sinners, spare?:‖

2 I have long withstood His grace;
 Long provoked Him to His face;
 Would not hearken to His calls,
 ‖: Grieved Him by a thousand falls. :‖

3 Now incline me to repent;
 Let me now my sins lament;
 Now my foul revolt deplore,
 ‖: Look, believe, and sin no more. :‖

195.

OUR Lord is now rejected,
    And by the world disowned,
By the *many* still neglected,
    And by the *few* enthroned;

But soon He'll come in glory,
  The hour is drawing nigh,
For the crowning day is coming by and by.

Cho.—Oh, the crowning day is coming,
    Is coming by and by,
  When our Lord shall come in
    " power "
  And " glory " from on high.
  Oh, the glorious sight will gladden,
    Each waiting, watchful eye,
  In the crowning day that's coming by
    and by.

2 The heavens shall glow with splendor,
    But brighter far than they
  The saints shall shine in glory,
    As Christ shall them array;
  The beauty of the Saviour
    Shall dazzle every eye,
  In the crowning day that's coming by and
    by.

3 Our pain shall then be over,
    We'll sin and sigh no more,
  Behind us all of sorrow,
    And nought but joy before;
  A joy in our Redeemer,
    As we to Him are nigh,
  In the crowning day that's coming by and
    by.

4 Let all that look for, hasten
    The coming joyful day,
  By earnest consecration,
    To walk the narrow way;
  By gathering in the lost ones,
    For whom our Lord did die,
  For the crowning day that's coming by
    and by.

196.

OH, tender and sweet was the Master's voice
As He lovingly called to me,
"Come over the line, it is only a step—
I am waiting, My child, for thee."

Ref.—"Over the line," hear the sweet refrain,
Angels are chanting the heavenly strain:
"Over the line,"—Why should I remain
With a step between me and Jesus?

2 But my sins are many, my faith is small,
Lo! the answer came quick and clear;
"Thou needest not trust thyself at all,
Step over the line, I am here."

3 But my flesh is weak, I tearfully said,
And the way I cannot see;
I fear if I try I may sadly fail,
And thus may dishonor Thee.

4 Ah, the world is cold, and I cannot go back,
Press forward I surely must;
I will place my hand in His wounded palm,
Step over the line, and *trust*.

Ref.—"Over the line," hear the sweet refrain,
Angels are chanting the heavenly strain;
"Over the line,"—*I will not* remain,
I'll cross it and go to Jesus.

197.

MORE love to Thee, O Christ!
More love to Thee;

Hear Thou the prayer I make,
 On bended knee;
This is my earnest plea,
More love, O Christ, to Thee,
‖: More love to Thee! :‖

2 Once earthly joy I craved,
 Sought peace and rest;
Now Thee alone I seek,
 Give what is best;
This all my prayer shall be,
More love, O Christ, to Thee.
‖: More love to Thee! :‖

3 Then shall my latest breath,
 Whisper Thy praise,
This be the parting cry
 My heart shall raise:
This still its prayer shall be:
More love, O Christ, to Thee
‖: More love to Thee! :‖

198.

LIGHT after darkness,
 Gain after loss,
Strength after weakness
 Crown after Cross;
Sweet after bitter,
 Hope after fears,
Home after wand'ring,
 Praise after tears.

2 Sheaves after sowing,
 Sun after rain,
Sight after mystery,
 Peace after pain;
Joy after sorrow,
 Calm after blast,
Rest after weariness
 Sweet rest at last.

3 Near after distant,
   Gleam after gloom,
Love after loneliness,
   Life after tomb;
After long agony,
   Rapture of bliss,
Right was the pathway,
   Leading to this.

199.

WHY do you wait, dear brother,
   Oh, why do you tarry so long?
Your Saviour is waiting to give you
   A place in His sanctified throng.

Cho.—Why not? why not?
   Why not come to Him now?
Why not? why not?
   Why not come to Him now?

2 What do you hope, dear brother,
   To gain by a further delay?
There's no one to save you but Jesus,
   There's no other way but His way.

3 Do you not feel, dear brother,
   His Spirit now striving within?
Oh, why not accept His salvation,
   And throw off thy burden of sin.

4 Why do you wait, dear brother,
   The harvest is passing away,
Your Saviour is longing to bless you,
   There's danger and death in delay.

200.

ROCK of Ages, cleft for me,
   Let me hide myself in Thee;
Let the water and the blood,
From Thy riven side which flow'd,

Be of sin the double cure,
  Save me from its guilt and pow'r.
2 Not the labor of my hands
  Can fulfill Thy law's demands;
  Could my zeal no respite know,
  Could my tears forever flow,
  All for sin could not atone;
  Thou must save, and Thou alone.
3 Nothing in my hand I bring,
  Simply to Thy cross I cling;
  Naked, come to Thee for dress,
  Helpless, look to Thee for grace;
  Foul, I to the fountain fly,
  Wash me, Saviour, or I die.
4 While I draw this fleeting breath,
  When mine eyes shall close in death,
  When I soar to worlds unknown,
  See Thee on Thy judgment throne—
  Rock of Ages, cleft for me,
  Let me hide myself in Thee.

201.
ALL hail the power of Jesus' name!
  Let angels prostrate fall,
||: Bring forth the royal diadem,
  And crown Him Lord of all.:||
2 Let every kindred, every tribe,
  On this terrestrial ball,
||: To Him all majesty ascribe,
  And crown Him Lord of all.:||
3 Oh, that with yonder sacred throng
  We at His feet may fall;
||: We'll join the everlasting song,
  And crown Him Lord of all.:||

202.
O FOR a thousand tongues to sing
  My great Redeemer's praise;

The glories of my God and King,
  The triumphs of His grace.

2 My gracious Master, and my God,
    Assist me to proclaim—
  To spread through all the earth abroad,
    The honors of Thy name.

3 Jesus!—the name that charms our fears,
    That bids our sorrows cease;
  'Tis music in the sinner's ears,
    'Tis life, and health, and peace.

4 He breaks the power of cancell'd sin,
    He sets the prisoner free;
  His blood can make the foulest clean;
    His blood availed for me.

203.

IN the cross of Christ I glory,
  Towering o'er the wrecks of time;
All the light of sacred story,
  Gathers round its head sublime.

2 When the woes of life o'ertake me,
    Hopes deceive and fears annoy,
  Never shall the cross forsake me;
    Lo! it glows with peace and joy.

3 When the sun of bliss is beaming
    Light and love upon my way,
  From the cross the radiance streaming,
    Adds new lustre to the day.

4 Bane and blessing, pain and pleasure,
    By the cross are sanctified;
  Peace is there, that knows no measure,
    Joys that through all time abide.

204.

AM I a soldier of the cross—
  A foll'wer of the Lamb,—

And shall I fear to own His cause,
  Or blush to speak His name?

2 Must I be carried to the skies
    On flow'ry beds of ease;
  While others fought to win the prize,
    And sail'd thro' bloody seas?

3 Are there no foes for me to face?
    Must I not stem the flood?
  Is this vile world a friend to grace,
    To help me on to God?

4 Since I must fight if I would reign,
    Increase my courage, Lord;
  I'll bear the toil, endure the pain,
    Supported by Thy word.

205.
AWAKE, my soul, stretch every nerve,
    And press with vigor on;
  A heavenly race demands thy zeal,
    And an immortal crown.

2 A cloud of witnesses around
    Hold thee in full survey;
  Forget the steps already trod,
    And onward urge thy way.

3 'Tis God's all-animating voice,
    That calls thee from on high,
  'Tis His own hand presents the prize
    To thine aspiring eye.

4 Blest Saviour, introduced by Thee
    Have I my race begun;
  And, crowned with victory, at Thy feet
    I'll lay my honors down.

206.
WHILE shepherds watched their flocks by night,
  All seated on the ground,

The angel of the Lord came down,
‖: And glory shone around.:‖

2 "Fear not" said he,—for mighty dread
   Had seized their troubled mind—,
"Glad tidings of great joy I bring,
 ‖: To you and all mankind.:‖

3 "To you, in David's town, this day,
   Is born of David's line,
The Saviour, who is Christ, the Lord,
 ‖: And this shall be the sign;—:‖

4 "The heavenly babe you there shall find
   To human view displayed,
All meanly wrapped in swathing bands,
 ‖: And in a manger laid." :‖

5 Thus spake the seraph—and forthwith
   Appeared a shining throng
Of angels, praising God, who thus
 ‖:Addressed their joyful song :—:‖

6 "All glory be to God on high,
   And to the earth be peace;
Good-will henceforth from heaven to men
 ‖: Begin, and never cease!":‖

207.

1 THE Lord's my Shepherd, I'll not want:
    He makes me down to lie
In pastures green: He leadeth me
    The quiet waters by.

2 My soul He doth restore again;
    And me to walk doth make
Within the paths of righteousness,
    E'en for His own name's sake.

3 Yea, tho' I walk in death's dark vale,
    Yet I will fear none ill;
For Thou art with me; and Thy rod
    And staff me comfort still.

4 My table Thou hast furnished
   In presence of my foes;
My head thou dost with oil anoint,
   And my cup overflows.

5 Goodness and mercy all my life
   Shall surely follow me;
And in God's house for evermore
   My dwelling-place shall be.

208.
COME, Holy Spirit, Heavenly Dove!
   With all Thy quickening powers,
Kindle a flame of sacred love
   In these cold hearts of ours.

2 Look! how we grovel here below,
   Fond of these trifling toys!
Our souls can neither fly nor go
   To reach eternal joys.

3 In vain we tune our formal songs;
   In vain we strive to rise;
Hosannas languish on our tongues,
   And our devotion dies.

4 Dear Lord, and shall we ever live
   At this poor dying rate—
Our love so faint, so cold to Thee,
   And Thine to us so great?

5 Come, Holy Spirit, Heavenly Dove!
   With all Thy quickening powers;
Come, shed abroad a Saviour's love,
   And that shall kindle ours.

209.
MUST Jesus bear the cross alone,
   And all the world go free?
No, there's a cross for every one,
   And there's a cross for me.

2 The consecrated cross I'll bear,
　　Till death shall set me free;
　And then go home my crown to wear,
　　For there's a crown for me.
3 Upon the crystal pavement, down
　　At Jesus pierc̄ed feet.
　Joyful, I'll cast my golden crown,
　　And His dear name repeat.
4 Oh, precious cross! oh, glorious crown!
　　Oh, resurrection day!
　Ye angels, from the stars come down,
　　And bear my soul away.

210.

I HEARD the voice of Jesus say,
　　"Come unto me and rest;
　Lay down, thou weary one, lay down
　　Thy head upon my breast."
2 I came to Jesus as I was—
　　Weary, and worn, and sad;
　I found in Him a resting-place,
　　And He has made me glad.
3 I heard the voice of Jesus say,
　　"Behold I freely give
　The living water—thirsty one,
　　Stoop down, and drink, and live."
4 I came to Jesus, and I drank
　　Of that life-giving stream;
　My thirst was quench'd, my soul revived
　　And now I live in Him.
5 I heard the voice of Jesus say,
　　"I am this dark world's light;
　Look unto me, thy morn shall rise,
　　And all thy day be bright."
6 I looked to Jesus, and I found
　　In Him my Star, my Sun;

And in that Light of Life I'll walk
Till trav'ling days are done.

211.

JUST as I am, without one plea,
  But that Thy blood was shed for me,
And that Thou bidd'st me come to Thee,
  O Lamb of God! I come, I come!

2 Just as I am, and waiting not
To rid my soul of one dark blot,
To Thee, whose blood can cleanse each spot,
  O Lamb of God! I come, I come!

3 Just as I am, though toss'd about,
With many a conflict, many a doubt,
Fightings and fears within, without,
  O Lamb of God! I come, I come!

4 Just as I am, poor, wretched, blind,
Sight, riches, healing of the mind,
Yea, all I need in Thee to find,
  O Lamb of God! I come, I come!

5 Just as I am: Thou wilt receive,
Wilt welcome, pardon, cleanse, relieve;
Because Thy promise I believe,
  O Lamb of God! I come, I come!

212.

WHEN I survey the wondrous cross,
  On which the Prince of glory died,
My richest gain I count but loss,
  And pour contempt on all my pride.

2 Forbid it, Lord! that I should boast,
  Save in the death of Christ, my God,
All the vain things that charm me most
  I sacrifice them to His blood.

3 See, from His head, His hands, His feet,
  Sorrow and love flow mingled down;

Did e'er such love and sorrow meet,
Or thorns compose so rich a crown?

4 His dying crimson, like a robe,
Spreads o'er His body on the tree;
Then I am dead to all the globe,
And all the globe is dead to me.

5 Were the whole realm of nature mine,
That were a present far too small;
Love so amazing, so divine,
Demands my soul, my life, my all.

213.

JESUS shall reign where'er the sun
Does his successive journeys run,
His kingdom spread from shore to shore,
Till moons shall wax and wane no more.

2 To Him shall endless prayer be made,
And praises throng to crown His head,
His name, like sweet perfume, shall rise
With every morning sacrifice.

3 People and realms of every tongue
Dwell on His love with sweetest song;
And infant voices shall proclaim
Their early blessings on His name.

4 Blessings abound where'er He reigns,
The prisoner leaps to loose his chains;
The weary find eternal rest,
And all the sons of want are blest.

5 Let every creature rise, and bring
Peculiar honors to our King:
Angels descend with songs again,
And earth repeat the long amen.

214.

NOT all the blood of beasts
On Jewish altars slain,

Could give the guilty conscience peace
　Or wash away the stain.

2 But Christ, the heav'nly Lamb,
　　Takes all our sins away;
　A sacrifice of nobler name,
　　And richer blood than they.

3 My faith would lay her hand
　　On that dear head of Thine,
　While like a penitent I stand,
　　And there confess my sin.

4 My soul looks back to see
　　The burden Thou didst bear:
　While hanging on the cursèd tree,
　　And knows her guilt was there.

215.

LORD, bless and pity us,
　　Shine on us with Thy face:
That th' earth Thy way, and nations all
　　May know Thy saving grace.

2 Let people praise Thee, Lord!
　　Let people all Thee praise!
　Oh, let the nations all be glad,
　　In songs their voices raise!

3 Thou'lt justly people judge,
　　On earth rule nations all:
　Let people praise Thee, Lord! let them
　　Praise Thee, both great and small!

4 The earth her fruit shall yield,
　　Our God shall blessings send;
　God shall us bless: men shall Him fear
　　Unto earth's utmost end.

216.

BLEST be the tie that binds
　　Our hearts in Christian love;

The fellowship of kindred minds
  Is like to that above.

2 Before our Father's throne,
    We pour our ardent prayers;
  Our fears, our hopes, our aims are one,—
    Our comforts and our cares.

3 We share our mutual woes;
    Our mutual burdens bear;
  And often for each other flows
    The sympathizing tear.

4 When we asunder part,
    It gives us inward pain;
  But we shall still be joined in heart,
    And hope to meet again.

217.

HOW firm a foundation, ye saints of the Lord!
Is laid for your faith in His excellent word!
What more can He say, than to you He hath said,—
||: To you, who for refuge to Jesus hath fled? :||

2 Fear not, I am with thee, oh, be not dismayed,
For I am thy God, I will still give thee aid;
I'll strengthen thee, help thee, and cause thee to stand,
||: Upheld by My gracious, omnipotent hand. :||

3 "When thro' the deep waters I call thee to go,
The rivers of sorrow shall not overflow;

For I will be with thee thy trouble to bless,
‖: And sanctify to thee thy deepest distress. :‖

4 " The soul that on Jesus hath leaned for repose,
I will not—I will not desert to His foes ;
That soul—tho' all hell should endeavor to shake,
‖: I'll never — no never — no never forsake ! :‖

218.

GLORY be to the Father, and to the Son,
and to the Holy Ghost ;
As it was in the beginning, is now, and ever shall be, world without end.
Amen, Amen.

219.

TAKE my life and let it be
Consecrated, Lord, to Thee ;
Take my hands and let them move
‖: At the impulse of Thy love. :‖

2 Take my feet and let them be
Swift and beautiful for Thee ;
Take my voice and let me sing
‖: Always—only—for my King. :‖

3 Take my lips and let them be
Fill'd with messages from Thee ;
Take my silver and my gold,
‖: Not a mite would I withhold. :‖

4 Take my moments and my days,
Let them flow in endless praise ;
Take my intellect and use
‖: Ev'ry pow'r as Thou shalt choose. :‖

11

5 Take my will and make it Thine,
  It shall be no longer mine;
  Take my heart, it is Thine own,
  ‖: It shall be Thy royal throne. :‖

6 Take my love, my God, I pour
  At thy feet its treasure-store
  Take myself, and I will be
  ‖: Ever, only, all for Thee. :‖

220.

COME, said Jesus' sacred voice,
  Come, and make my paths your choice;
I will guide you to your home,
Weary pilgrim, hither come!

2 Thou who, houseless, sole, forlorn,
  Long hast borne the proud world's scorn,
  Long hast roamed the barren waste,
  Weary pilgrim, hither haste.

3 Ye who, tossed on beds of pain,
  Seek for ease, but seek in vain;
  Ye, by fiercer anguish torn,
  In remorse for guilt who mourn;—

4 Hither come! for here is found
  Balm that flows for every wound,
  Peace that ever shall endure,
  Rest eternal, sacred, sure.

221.

SINNERS, turn, why will ye die!
  God, your Maker, asks you—why?
God, who did your being give,
Made you with Himself to live;
He the fatal cause demands,
Asks the work of His own hands,—

Why, ye thankless creatures, why
Will ye cross His love, and die?

2 Sinners, turn, why will ye die?
God, your Saviour, asks you—why?
He who did your souls retrieve,
Died Himself that ye might live,
Will ye let Him die in vain?
Crucify your Lord again?
Why, ye ransomed sinners, why
Will ye slight His grace, and die?

3 Sinners, turn, why will ye die?
God, the Spirit, asks you—why?
He, who all your lives hath strove,
Urged you to embrace His love:
Will you not His grace receive?
Will ye still refuse to live?
Why, ye long-sought sinners! why,
Will ye grieve your God, and die?

222.

JESUS, Lover of my soul,
   Let me to Thy bosom fly,
While the nearer waters roll,
   While the tempest still is high;
Hide me, oh, my Saviour hide,
   Till the storm of life is past;
Safe into the haven guide,
   Oh, receive my soul at last.

2 Other refuge have I none,
   Hangs my helpless soul on Thee;
Leave, oh, leave me not alone,
   Still support and comfort me:
All my trust on Thee is stayed,
   All my help from Thee I bring;
Cover my defenceless head
   With the shadow of Thy wing.

3 Thou, O Christ, art all I want;
  More than all in Thee I find:
Raise the fallen, cheer the faint,
  Heal the sick and lead the blind:
Just and holy is Thy name,
  I am all unrighteousness;
Vile, and full of sin I am,
  Thou art full of truth and grace.

4 Plenteous grace with Thee is found—
  Grace to cover all my sin;
Let the healing streams abound;
  Make me, keep me, pure within,
Thou of life the Fountain art,
  Freely let me take of Thee;
Spring Thou up within my heart,
  Rise to all eternity.

223.

NEARER, my God, to Thee,
  Nearer to Thee;
E'en though it be a cross
  That raiseth me,
Still all my song shall be—
‖: Nearer, my God, to Thee! :‖
  Nearer to Thee!

2 Tho', like a wanderer,
  The sun gone down,
Darkness be over me,
  My rest a stone,
Yet in my dreams I'd be
‖: Nearer, my God, to Thee! :‖
  Nearer to Thee!

3 There let the way appear
  Steps unto heaven;
All that Thou sendest me,
  In mercy given:

Angels to beckon me
‖: Nearer, my God, to Thee ! :‖
Nearer to Thee !

4 Then with my waking tho'ts,
   Bright with Thy praise,
Out of my stony griefs,
   Bethel I'll raise ;
So by my woes to be
‖: Nearer, my God, to Thee ! :‖
Nearer to Thee !

5 Or if, on joyful wing,
   Cleaving the sky,
Sun, moon, and stars forgot,
   Upward I fly,
Still all my song shall be
‖: Nearer, my God, to Thee ! :‖
Nearer to Thee !

224.

WORK, for the night is coming,
   Work thro' the morning hours ;
Work while the dew is sparkling,
   Work 'mid springing flow'rs ;
Work, when the day grows brighter,
   Work in the glowing sun ;
Work, for the night is coming,
   When man's work is done.

2 Work, for the night is coming,
   Work through the sunny noon;
Fill brightest hours with labor,
   Rest comes sure and soon,
Give every flying minute,
   Something to keep in store ;
Work, for the night is coming,
   When man works no more.

3 Work, for the night is coming,
   Under the sunset skies;
While their bright tints are glowing,
   Work, for daylight flies,
Work till the last beam fadeth,
   Fadeth to shine no more;
Work while the night is darkening,
   When man's work is o'er.

225.

THERE is a fountain filled with blood,
   Drawn from Immanuel's veins;
And sinners plunged beneath that flood,
   Lose all their guilty stains.

2 The dying thief rejoiced to see
   That fountain in his day;
And there may I, though vile as he,
   Wash all my sins away.

3 Dear dying Lamb, Thy precious blood
   Shall never lose its power,
Till all the ransomed church of God
   Be saved to sin no more.

4 E'er since, by faith, I saw the stream
   Thy flowing wounds supply,
Redeeming love has been my theme,
   And shall be, till I die.

5 Then in a nobler, sweeter song,
   I'll sing Thy power to save,
When this poor lisping, stammering tongue
   Lies silent in the grave.

226.

STAND up!—stand up for Jesus!
   Ye soldiers of the cross;
Lift high His royal banner,
   It must not suffer loss:

From vict'ry unto vict'ry
　His army shall He lead,
Till ev'ry foe is vanquished,
　And Christ is Lord indeed.

2 Stand up!—stand up for Jesus!
　　The trumpet call obey;
　Forth to the mighty conflict,
　　In this His glorious day:
　" Ye that are men, now serve Him,"
　　Against unnumbered foes:
　Let courage rise with danger,
　　And strength to strength oppose.

3 Stand up!—stand up for Jesus!
　　Stand in His strength alone;
　The arm of flesh will fail you—
　　Ye dare not trust your own;
　Put on the gospel armor,
　　And, watching unto prayer,
　Where duty calls, or danger,
　　Be never wanting there.

4 Stand up!—stand up for Jesus!
　　The strife will not be long;
　This day, the noise of battle,
　　The next, the victor's song:
　To him that overcometh,
　　A crown of life shall be;
　He with the King of glory
　　Shall reign eternally!

227.

THE morning light is breaking,
　The darkness disappears!
The sons of earth are waking
　To penitential tears;
Each breeze that sweeps the ocean
　Brings tidings from afar,

Of nations in commotion,
  Prepared for Zion's war.

2 See heathen nations bending
    Before the God we love,
  And thousand hearts ascending
    In gratitude above;
  While sinners, now confessing,
    The gospel call obey,
  And seek the Saviour's blessing—
    A nation in a day.

3 Blest river of salvation!
    Pursue thine onward way;
  Flow thou to every nation,
    Nor in thy richness stay:
  Stay not till all the lowly
    Triumphant reach their home:
  Stay not till all the holy
    Proclaim—"The Lord is come!"

228.

SOMETIMES a light surprises
    The Christian while he sings;
  It is the Lord who rises
    With healing in His wings:
  When comforts are declining,
    He grants the soul again
  A season of clear shining,
    To cheer it after rain.

2 In holy contemplation,
    We sweetly then pursue
  The theme of God's salvation,
    And find it ever new:
  Set free from present sorrow,
    We cheerfully can say,
  Let the unknown to-morrow
    Bring with it what it may.

3 It can bring with it nothing,
   But He will bring us through;
Who gives the lilies clothing,
   Will clothe His people, too:
Beneath the spreading heavens,
   No creature but is fed;
And He who feeds the ravens,
   Will give His children bread.

4 Though vine nor fig-tree neither,
   Their wonted fruit shall bear,
Though all the fields should wither,
   Nor flocks, nor herds be there;
Yet God the same abiding,
   His praise shall tune my voice,
For while in Him confiding,
   I cannot but rejoice.

229.

MY faith looks up to Thee,
   Thou Lamb of Calvary,
    Saviour divine!
Now hear me while I pray,
Take all my guilt away,
Oh, let me from this day
    Be wholly Thine!

2 May Thy rich grace impart
   Strength to my fainting heart,
    My zeal inspire;
As Thou hast died for me,
Oh, may my love to Thee
Pure, warm, and changeless be—
    A living fire.

3 While life's dark maze I tread,
   And griefs around me spread,
    Be Thou my guide;

Bid darkness turn to day,
Wipe sorrow's tears away,
Nor let me ever stray
  From Thee aside.

4 When ends life's transient dream,
When death's cold, sullen stream
  Shall o'er me roll,
Blest Saviour! then, in love,
Fear and distrust remove;
Oh, bear me safe above,
  A ransomed soul.

230.

JESUS, Thy name I love,
  All other names above,
    Jesus, my Lord!
Oh, Thou art all to me!
Nothing to please I see,
Nothing apart from Thee,
    Jesus, my Lord!

2 Thou, blessèd Son of God,
Hast bought me with Thy blood,
    Jesus, my Lord!
Oh, how great is Thy love,
All other loves above!
Love that I daily prove,
    Jesus, my Lord!

3 When unto Thee I flee,
Thou wilt my refuge be,
    Jesus, my Lord!
What need I now to fear?
What earthly grief or care,
Since Thou art ever near?
    Jesus, my Lord!

4 Soon Thou wilt come again!
I shall be happy then,
  Jesus, my Lord!
Then Thine own face I'll see,
Then I shall like Thee be,
Then evermore with Thee,
  Jesus, my Lord!

231.
Come, Thou Almighty King,
  Help us Thy name to sing,
    Help us to praise:
Father! all-glorious,
O'er all victorious,
Come, and reign over us,
    Ancient of Days!

2 Come, Thou incarnate Word,
  Gird on Thy mighty sword;
    Our prayer attend:
Come, and Thy people bless,
And give Thy word success:
Spirit of Holiness!
    On us descend.

3 Come, Holy Comforter!
  Thy sacred witness bear,
    In this glad hour:
Thou, who almighty art,
Now rule in every heart,
And ne'er from us depart,
    Spirit of power!

4 To the great One in Three,
  The highest praises be,
    Hence evermore!
His sovereign majesty
May we in glory see,
And to eternity
    Love and adore.

232.

SOUND, sound the truth abroad,
  Bear ye the word of God
    Through the wide world:
Tell what our Lord has done,
Tell how the day is won,
And from His lofty throne
    Satan is hurled.

2 Speed on the wings of love,
Jesus, who reigns above,
    Bids us to fly;
They who His message bear
Should neither doubt nor fear,
He will their Friend appear,
    He will be nigh.

3 Ye, who forsaking all,
At your loved Master's call,
    Comforts resign;
Soon will your work be done;
Soon will the prize be won;
Brighter than yonder sun
    Then shall ye shine.

233.

RISE, glorious Conqueror, rise
  Into Thy native skies,—
    Assume Thy right;
And where in many a fold
The clouds are backward rolled—
Pass through those gates of gold,
    And reign in light!

2 Victor o'er death and hell!
Cherubic legions swell
    Thy radiant train:

Praises all heaven inspire;
Each angel sweeps his lyre,
And waves his wings of fire,—
 Thou Lamb once slain!

3 Enter, incarnate God!—
No feet but Thine have trod
 The serpent down;
Blow the full trumpets, blow;
Wider yon portals throw!
Saviour triumphant—go,
 And take Thy crown!

4 Lion of Judah—hail!
And let Thy name prevail
 From age to age;
Lord of the rolling years!
Claim for Thine own the spheres,
For Thou hast bought with tears
 Thy heritage.

5 And then was heard afar
Star answering to star—
 "Lo! these have come,
Followers of Him who gave
His life their lives to save;
And now their palms they wave,
 Brought safely home."

234.

MY country 'tis of thee,
 Sweet land of liberty,
 Of thee I sing;
Land where my fathers died,
Land of the pilgrim's pride,
From every mountain side,
 Let freedom ring.

2 My native country, thee,
   Land of the noble free,
      Thy name I love;
   I love thy rocks and rills,
   Thy woods and templed hills,
   My heart with rapture thrills,
      Like that above.

3 Let music swell the breeze,
   And ring from all the trees
      Sweet freedom's song;
   Let mortal tongues awake,
   Let all that breathe partake,
   Let rocks their silence break,
      The sound prolong.

4 Our fathers' God, to Thee,
   Author of liberty,
      To Thee we sing;
   Long may our land be bright,
   With freedom's holy light,
   Protect us by Thy might,
      Great God, our King!

INDEX.

First Lines in Roman. Titles in Small Capitals refer only to Music Edition.

A

	NO.
Abide with Me, fast falls the	51
ABUNDANTLY ABLE TO SAVE	122
ADRIAN. S. M.	111
Afflictions, tho' they seem	60
A guilty soul, by Pharisees of old	120
AHIRA. S. M.	109
Alas! and did my Saviour bleed	39
All hail the power of Jesus' name	201
All to Christ I owe	172
Almost persuaded	153
AMERICA. 6, 4	234
Am I a soldier of the cross	204
ANTIOCH. C. M.	190
Are you ready, are you ready	24
ARLINGTON. C. M.	204
A SHELTER IN THE TIME OF STORM	55
A SINNER LIKE ME	117
As I wandered round the home	78
AT THE CROSS	39
At the feast of Belshazzar	114
Awake, my soul, stretch every	205
Awake, my soul, to joyful lays	142
Awake, my soul! to sound His praise	35

B

Behold a fountain deep and wide	6
Behold, what love!	164
BELIEVE, AND KEEP ON BELIEVING	21
BELMONT. C. M.	207
BELOVED, NOW ARE WE	94
BEMERTON. C. M.	47

	NO.
BETHANY. 6, 4	223
BEULAH LAND	192
BE YE ALSO READY	24
Be ye strong in the Lord	92
Beyond the smiling and the weeping	186
Blessed assurance, Jesus is mine	38
Blessed be the fountain	96
Blest be the tie that binds	216
BOYLSTON. S. M	214
BRINGING IN THE SHEAVES	193
BUT IS THAT ALL?	132

C

CALVARY	90
CARRIED BY THE ANGELS	124
CASTING ALL YOUR CARE UPON HIM	61
Choose I must, and soon must choose	137
CHRIST AROSE	57
Christian, walk carefully	133
Christ is coming, let creation	189
CHRISTMAS. C. M	206
CHRIST RECEIVETH SINFUL MEN	65
Cling to the Bible tho' all else	127
Closer, Lord, to Thee	11
CLOSE TO THEE	183
Come, come to Jesus!	123
Come, ev'ry soul by sin oppressed	171
COME, GREAT DELIVERER, COME	73
Come, Holy Spirit, Heavenly Dove	208
Come, Praise the Lord, exalt His name	131
Come, said Jesus' sacred voice	220
COME, SINNER, COME	145
Come, Thou Almighty King	231
Come to Jesus, come away	113
COME TO THE FOUNTAIN	7
Come to the Saviour, hear His loving	139
Come unto Me, it is the Saviour's	88
Come we that love the Lord	151
Come with thy sins to the fountain	7
CORONATION. C. M	201

D

DENNIS. S. M	216
Depth of mercy can it be	194

INDEX.

	NO.
Down in the valley with my Saviour	148
DUKE ST. L. M.	213

E

ETERNITY	187
EVENING PRAYER	41
EVERY DAY WILL I BLESS THEE	1

F

Far, far away in heathen darkness	27
Fear not, God is thy shield	48
FEAR THOU NOT	125
FOLLOW ON	148
"For God so loved;" oh, wondrous	63

G

Gather them in, for there yet	150
GEER. C. M.	95
GIVE ME THINE HEART	19
GLORIA PATRI	87
Glory be to the Father	87, 218
Glory ever be to Jesus	15
GLORY TO GOD, THE FATHER	63
God be with you till we meet	74
God calling yet, shall I not	110
"God is love," His word proclaims	12
God loved a world of sinners	112
God's almighty arms are round me	76
GOD'S TIME NOW	137
GO YE INTO ALL THE WORLD	27
Guide me, O Thou great Jehovah	129

H

HALLELUJAH FOR THE CROSS	135
Hark! hark! my soul! angelic	128
HAVE COURAGE, MY BOY, TO SAY NO!	136
Have faith in God, what can	105
Have our hearts grown cold since	126
Have you any room for Jesus?	152
He holds the key of all unknown	134

INDEX.

	NO.
He is coming, the "Man of Sorrows"	18
HENDON. 7s., 4 lines	219
HIDING IN THEE	158
Hold thou my hand, so weak	91
Ho, reapers in the whitened	81
How firm a foundation, ye saints of	217
How SHALL we ESCAPE?	112
HOW SWEET MY SAVIOUR TO REPOSE	61

I

I am far frae my hame	191
I AM PRAYING FOR YOU	17
I AM THE WAY	104
I am Thine, O Lord!	156
I believe in God's wonderful	21
IF GOD BE FOR US	9
I gave My life for thee	184
I have a Saviour, He's pleading in	173
I heard the voice of Jesus say	210
I hear the Saviour say	172
I hear Thy welcome voice	179
I know I love Thee better, Lord	28
I know not why God's wondrous	5
I know that my Redeemer lives	32
I KNOW WHOM I HAVE BELIEVED	5
I looked to Jesus in my sin	67
I must walk thro' the valley	75
I need Thee every hour	181
In the cross of Christ I glory	203
In the harvest-field there is	62
IN THE HOLLOW OF HIS HAND	3
In the land of strangers	71
In the secret of His presence	98
In the shadow of His wings	40
I SHALL BE SATISFIED	174
ITALIAN HYMN. 6, 4	231
IT IS WELL WITH MY SOUL	157
I've found a friend in Jesus	102
I've found a Friend, oh, such a Friend	168
I've reached the land of corn and wine	192
I was once far away from the	117
I WILL	68
I will sing of my Redeemer	161
I will sing the wondrous story	114

J

	NO.
Jerusalem, my happy home	115
Jesus bids us shine with a	121
JESUS CHRIST, OUR SAVIOUR	16
JESUS, I COME	14
JESUS IS CALLING	42
Jesus is tenderly calling thee	42
Jesus, keep me near the cross	182
Jesus knows thy sorrow	149
Jesus, Lover of my soul	222
Jesus, my Lord, to Thee I cry	69
Jesus, my Saviour, to Bethlehem	14
JESUS SAVES!	17
Jesus, Saviour, pilot me	101
Jesus shall reign where'er the sun	213
Jesus, the very thought of Thee	108
Jesus, Thy name I love	230
JEWETT, 6s, 8 lines	107
JOY COMETH IN THE MORNING	23
Joy to the world! the Lord is come	190
Just as I am, without one plea	211

L

Laborers of Christ, arise	109
LABOR ON	62
LET THE SAVIOUR IN	66
Let us sing of the love of the Lord	45
Light after darkness	198
Like wandering sheep, o'er	104
LITTLE LIGHTS	121
Look unto Me, and be ye saved	77
Lord, bless and pity us	215
LOVING KINDNESS. L. M	142
Low in the grave He lay	57
LYTE, 6s, 4s	231

M

MANOAH. C. M	110
MARTYN. 7s, 8 lines	221
Meet me there	22
MIGHTY TO SAVE	56
More holiness give me	178
More love to Thee, O Christ	197
Must Jesus bear the cross alone	209

INDEX.

	NO.
MY AIN COUNTRIE	191
My country, 'tis of thee	234
My faith looks up to Thee	229
My Father is rich in houses and lands	36
My Jesus, as Thou wilt	107
My Jesus, I love Thee, I know	170
MY MOTHER'S PRAYER	78
MY PRAYER	178
MY REDEEMER	161
My Saviour's praises I will sing	1

N

Nearer, my God, to Thee	223
"Nearer the cross!" my heart	54
NEAR THE CROSS	182
Neither do I condemn thee	83
Not all the blood of beasts	214
Not far, not far from the kingdom	33
Now the day is over	97
NUMBERLESS AS THE SANDS	50

O

O brother! life's journey beginning	46
O child of God, wait patiently	8
O Christian traveler! fear no more	125
O for a thousand tongues to sing	202
O God, our help in ages past	47
O golden day, O day of God	140
Oh, cease, my wandering soul	111
Oh, hear the joyful message	86
Oh, soul, tossed on the billow	3
Oh, tender and sweet was the	196
Oh, the clanging bells of time	187
Oh, weary pilgrim, lift your head	23
Oh, what will you do with Jesus	108
Oh, where are the reapers?	159
Oh, who is this that cometh?	56
Oh, wonderful, wonderful word of	79
Oh, wondrous name, by prophets	44
O land of the Blessed	53
O list to the voice of the Prophet	20
OLIVET, 6, 4	229
O MORNING LAND	138

INDEX.

	NO.
On Calvary's brow my Saviour died	90
Once more, my soul, thy Saviour	68
Only a beam of sunshine	34
ONLY TRUST HIM	171
On that bright and golden morning	72
On the Resurrection morning	93
Onward, Christian soldiers	100
Onward, upward, homeward	2
O PARADISE	140
O, praise the Lord with heart	52
O precious word that Jesus said	29
O safe to the Rock that is higher	158
O THE CROWN, THE GLORY CROWN	30
O troubled heart, there is a home	64
Our Lord is now rejected	195
Out of my bondage, sorrow and	14
OVER THE LINE	196
O wandering souls, why will	59
O WHAT A SAVIOUR	139
O wonderful words of the gospel	10

P

PARDON, PEACE, AND POWER,	82
Pass me not, O gentle Saviour	169
PEACE, PEACE IS MINE	76
PILOT, 7s, 6 lines	101
PORTUGUESE HYMN, 11s	217
Praise Him! praise Him!	4
Praise the Saviour, ye who know	25

R

RATHBUN. 8, 7	203
REDEMPTION	101
REFUGE, 7, D	222
REJOICE IN THE LORD ALWAY	52
Rejoice in the Lord, oh! let His mercy	9
Rejoice, rejoice, believer	85
REPENT YE	126
Rescue the perishing	176
RESURRECTION MORN	93
Revive Thy work, O Lord	155
Rise, glorious Conqueror, rise	233
Rock of Ages, cleft for me	200

S

	NO.
Safe home, safe home in port	89
Saviour, again to Thy dear name	147
Saviour, breathe an evening blessing	41
Saviour, more than life to me	177
Saviour, Thy dying love	175
SEEKING FOR ME	13
SHALL YOU? SHALL I?	43
Shine on, O star of beauty	26
Simply trusting every day	165
Sing them over again to me	163
Sinners Jesus will receive	65
Sinners, turn, why will ye die?	221
Sitting by the gateway	124
Softly and tenderly Jesus is calling	58
Some day we say, and turn our eyes	138
Some one will enter the pearly	43
SOME SWEET DAY BY AND BY	106
SOMETHING FOR JESUS	175
Sometimes a light surprises	228
Sometimes I catch sweet glimpses	132
Songs of gladness, never sadness	37
Sons of God, beloved in Jesus	94
Soul of mine, in earthly temple	174
Souls of men, why will ye scatter	70
Sound, sound the truth abroad	232
Sowing in the morning	193
ST. AGNES. C. M	103
Stand up, stand up for Jesus	226
ST. PETER. C. M	35

T

TAKE ME AS I AM	69
Take my life, and let it be	219
THE BANNER OF THE CROSS	116
THE CHILD OF A KING	36
THE CLEANSING FOUNTAIN	6
The cross it standeth fast	135
THE CROWNING DAY	195
THE GOSPEL CALL	144
THE HANDWRITING ON THE WALL	114
THE LILY OF THE VALLEY	102
The Lord's my Shepherd, I'll not want	207
The Lord's our Rock, in Him	55

INDEX.

	NO.
THE LOVE THAT GAVE JESUS TO DIE	45
THE MODEL CHURCH	143
The morning light is breaking	227
THE NINETY AND NINE	154
THE PRODIGAL'S RETURN	60
THE SWEETEST NAME	80
There are lonely hearts to cherish	162
There is a calm beyond life's	118
There is a fountain filled with blood	225
There is a green hill far away	185
There is a name I love to hear	95
There is a stream whose gentle flow	119
There is no name so sweet	80
THERE IS NONE RIGHTEOUS	120
There's a royal banner given	116
There's a Stranger at the door	66
There shall be showers of blessing	49
There were ninety and nine	154
The Spirit and the bride say "Come"	144
THE SWEETEST NAME	80
THEY THAT BE WISE	20
THEY THAT WAIT UPON THE LORD	81
Though your sins be as scarlet	84
Thou, my everlasting portion	183
THROUGH THE VALLEY AND THE	75
"Till He come!" oh, let the words	99
'Tis the blessed hour of prayer	180
To the work, to the work	160
TRUSTING JESUS, THAT IS ALL	165

W

WAIT AND MURMUR NOT	64
WAITING FOR THE PROMISE	130
WARD, L. M.	119
Weary gleaner in the field	30
WEBB, 7, 6, 8 lines	226
We bow our knees unto the Father	130
We have heard the joyful sound	17
WELCOME, WANDERER, WELCOME	71
We lift our songs to Thee	31
Well, wife, I've found the model church	143
WE'RE MARCHING TO ZION	151
We shall meet beyond the river	188
WE SHALL MEET BY AND BY	188

INDEX.

	NO.
We shall reach the summer-land	106
What a friend we have in Jesus	167
WHAT A GATHERING	72
WHAT WILL YOU DO WITH JESUS	108
When I survey the wondrous cross	212
When peace like a river	157
When the mists have rolled in	146
When we gather at last over Jordan	50
Wherever we may go, by night	19
While Jesus whispers to you	145
While shepherds watched their flocks	206
WHILE THE DAYS ARE GOING BY	162
Who came down from heaven to earth	16
Whoever receiveth the Crucified	122
WHOEVER WILL	59
WHOSOEVER CALLETH	86
Why do you wait, dear brother!	199
WONDERFUL WORDS OF LIFE	163
WOODWORTH. L. M	211
Work, for the night is coming	224
Would we be joyful in the Lord	28

Y

Yield not to temptation	166
You're starting, my boy, on life's journey	136

A List of the Various Editions of
GOSPEL HYMNS.

GOSPEL HYMNS No. 6, WITH STANDARD SELECTIONS.

No. 6 is the latest of the Series, but will not be combined or bound up with the other volumes

WORDS AND MUSIC.

	By mail, postpaid, per copy.	By express, charges not prepaid, per 100.
Board Covers	35	$30 00
Flexible Cloth	55	50 00

WORDS ONLY.

Paper Covers	06	5 00
Board Covers	11	10 00
Cloth Covers, Gilt Stamp	16	15 00

NOTICE.—Nos. 1, 2, 3, 4 and 5, issued separately in same styles and prices as above.

Gospel Hymns COMBINED.

Embracing Nos. 1, 2 and 3—Without Duplicates.

WORDS AND MUSIC.

Board Covers	70	$60 00
Limp Cloth	85	75 00

WORDS ONLY.

Board Covers	17	15 00
Cloth Covers, large type	55	50 00

CORNET EDITIONS,
Containing the melodies only.

Gospel Hymns Consolidated.	Gospel Hymns No. 5.*
Paper Covers. Each $1 05	Paper Covers. Each $0 80
Cloth " . " 1 55	Cloth " " 1 05

* GOSPEL HYMNS No. 6, in same styles and prices.

LIST OF PRICES.

WORDS AND MUSIC.

	By Mail, Per Copy.	By Express, Charges not prepaid, per 100.
GOSPEL HYMNS Nos. 1, 2, 3, 4, 5* & 6*, published separately, each, Bds..	$0.35	$30.00

WORDS ONLY OF EACH OF THE ABOVE NUMBERS:

Paper Covers,	.06	5.00
Board Covers,	.11	10.00

Christian Endeavor Edition of No. 6.

Words and Music, boards,	.40	35.00
Words Only, boards,	.15	12.00

Gospel Hymns Consolidated.

CONTAINING NOS. 1, 2, 3 AND 4 IN ONE VOLUME.

WORDS AND MUSIC.

Boards, Small Type,	.50	45.00
*Boards, Large Type,	.85	75.00
Cloth, Large Type,	1.10	100.00

WORDS ONLY.

Paper Covers, Small Type,	.06	5.00
Cloth Covers, Small Type,	.11	10.00
Board Covers, Large Type,	.22	20.00
Stiff Cloth Covers, Large Type,	.27	25.00

* Issued also in SEVEN CHARACTER NOTES at same prices.

Evangeliums-Lieder.

(GERMAN GOSPEL HYMNS.)

Music Edition, Boards,	.46	40.00
Words Edition, Boards,	.17	15.00

Cornet Editions.

	By Mail. Per Copy.
†GOSPEL HYMNS No. 5, Paper Covers,	$0.80
" " " Cloth Covers	1.05
†No. 6 issued in same styles and prices.	
GOSPEL HYMNS CONSOLIDATED, Paper Covers,	1.05
" " " Cloth Covers,	1.55

A full Catalogue of all Styles and Prices sent on request.

THE BIGLOW & MAIN CO.	THE JOHN CHURCH CO.
76 East 9th St., New York.	74 W. 4th St., Cincinnati.
81 Randolph St., Chicago.	13 E. 16th St., New York.

FOR SALE BY ALL MUSIC DEALERS AND BOOKSELLERS.

www.ingramcontent.com/pod-product-compliance
Lightning Source LLC
Chambersburg PA
CBHW032147160426
43197CB00008B/807